Capturing the Castle

Images of Preston Castle
(2006-2016)

Angelica R. Jackson

Crow & Pitcher Press
California

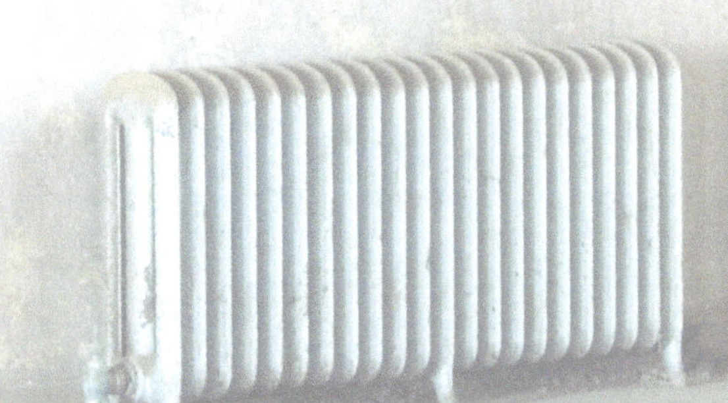

Crow & Pitcher Press

P.O. Box 1294

Shingle Springs, CA 95682-1294

www.crowandpitcherpress.com

Publisher's Cataloging-in-Publication data

Jackson, Angelica R.

Capturing the Castle : Images of Preston Castle (2006-2016)/Angelica R. Jackson.

p. cm.

ISBN 978-0-9987214-0-8

1. Photography —General. 2. Photographs —Collections. 3. Architecture —Public Buildings.

I. Jackson, Angelica R. II. Capturing the Castle: Images of Preston Castle (2006-2016)

Library of Congress Control Number: 2017902941

On a road trip some years ago, I took a shortcut through California's Gold Country and its former boomtowns. The peeling storefronts and decaying Victorian glamor began to blur through the window, until we approached the town of Ione.

On a hilltop, there stood an unlikely castle with fanciful turrets and a soaring clock tower, with its ruddy bricks warmed by the afternoon light. It was years before I would learn this was Preston Castle, formerly known as the Preston School of Industry, which operated as a youth correctional facility from 1894 through 1960.

Fascinated by this unique building, which had apparently been left to decay, I have photographed its interior over a ten-year period, and learned something of its history.

Inmates of San Quentin and Folsom furnished the bricks for the exterior, accented with red sandstone from local quarries. The Castle's main building functioned as offices, living quarters, and reception areas for the administrators.

The boys (called "wards" instead of the harsher term "prisoners") lived in the attached annex, divided into companies in military fashion. The annex building included a stark dormitory, a dining hall (which was later converted to an infirmary), and a basement day room with shower and bathroom.

The basement of the Castle housed the early group of wards until the annex was built. It was then put to various uses through the years, such as a day room, classroom, place of worship (thus the painted border of crosses), and storage.

Despite some of the successful wards that came out of the Castle, the State abandoned the Castle in 1960 and slated it for demolition. The doors to the doomed building were opened to the public, allowing people to salvage fixtures and furnishings. Elaborate mantels, light fixtures, and even a spiral staircase (now gracing the Firehouse Restaurant in Old Sacramento) were carted away. The Castle itself, after a long battle, was given a stay of execution and is still a beloved landmark in Ione.

The Preston Castle Foundation has been working to preserve and restore the Castle. See their website at www.PrestonCastle.com for more information and updates.

--Angelica R. Jackson

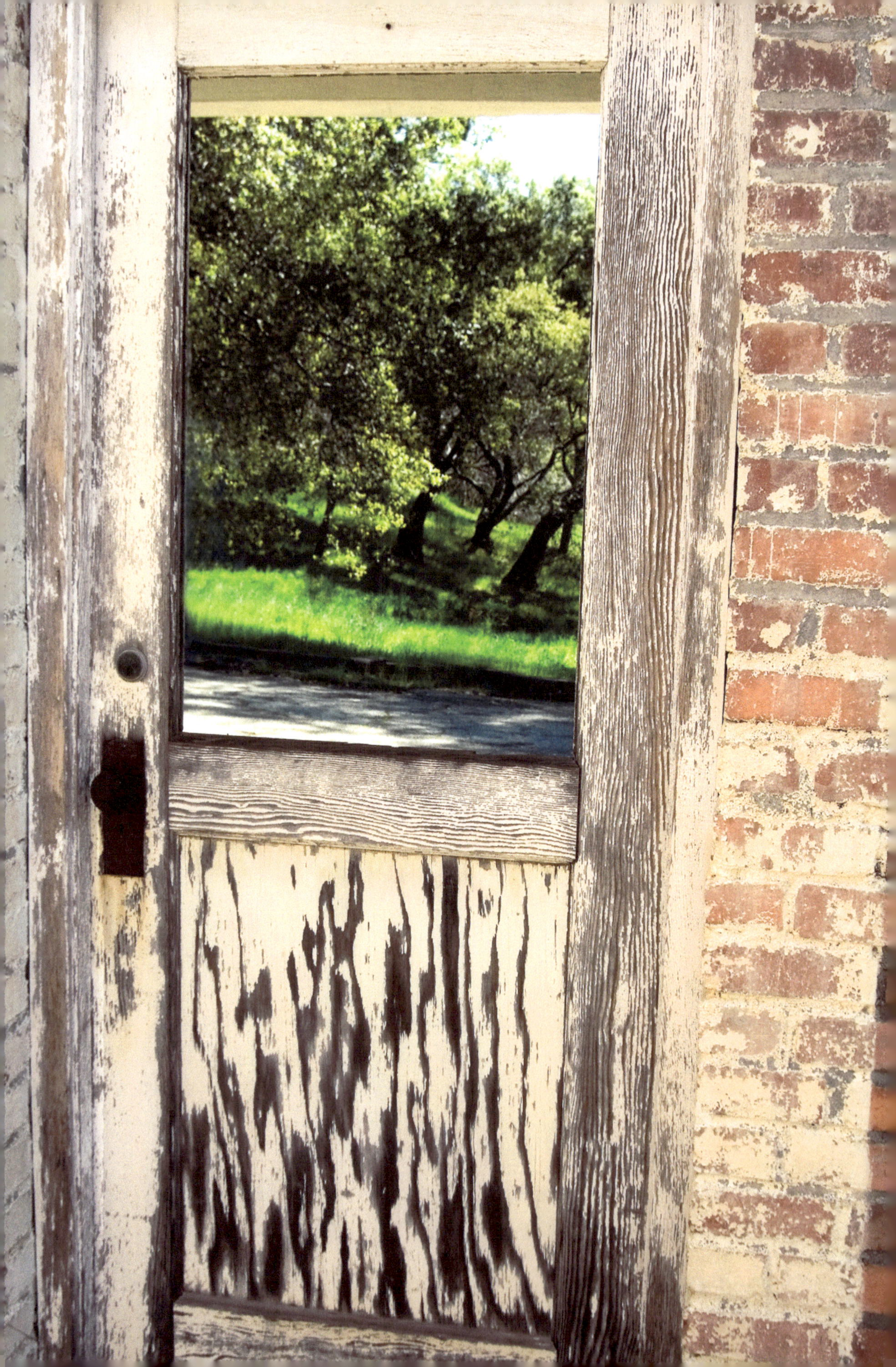

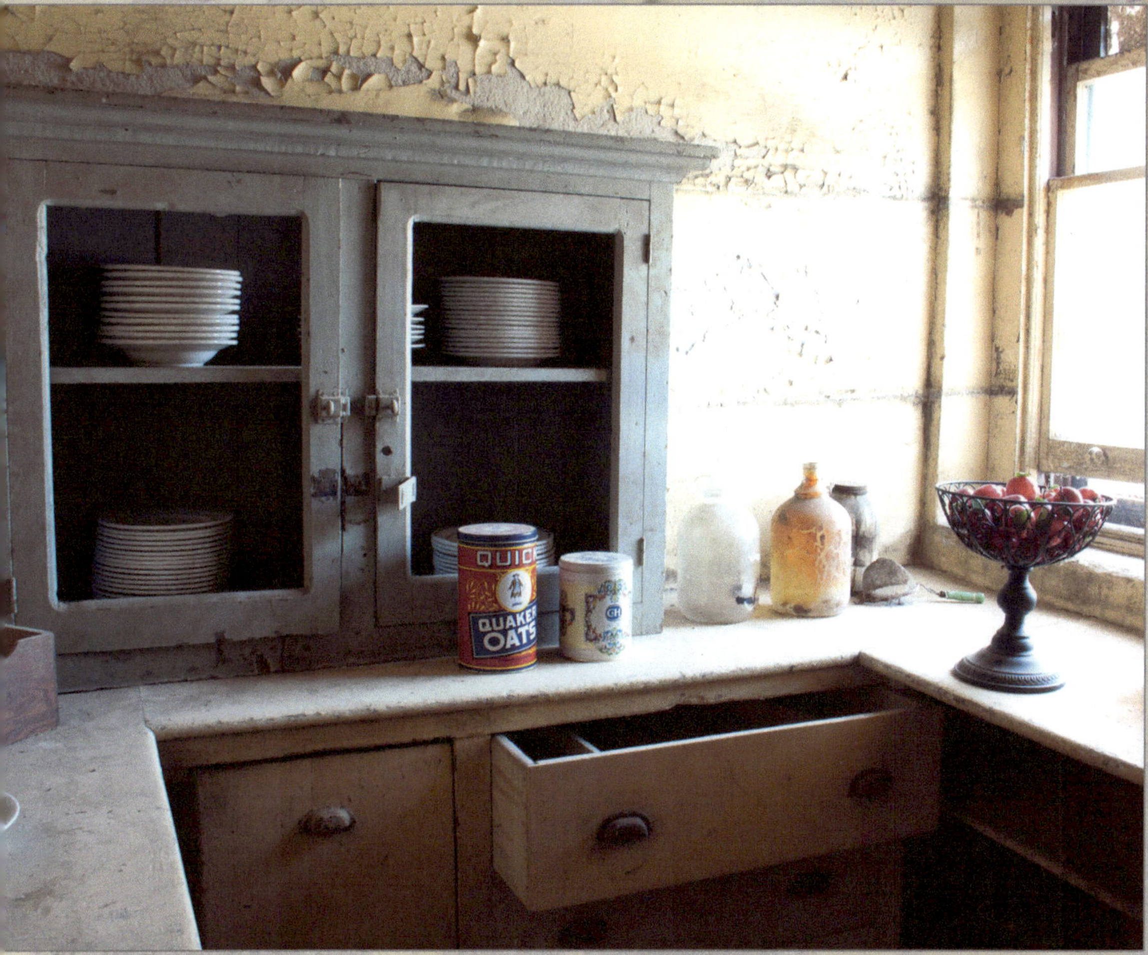

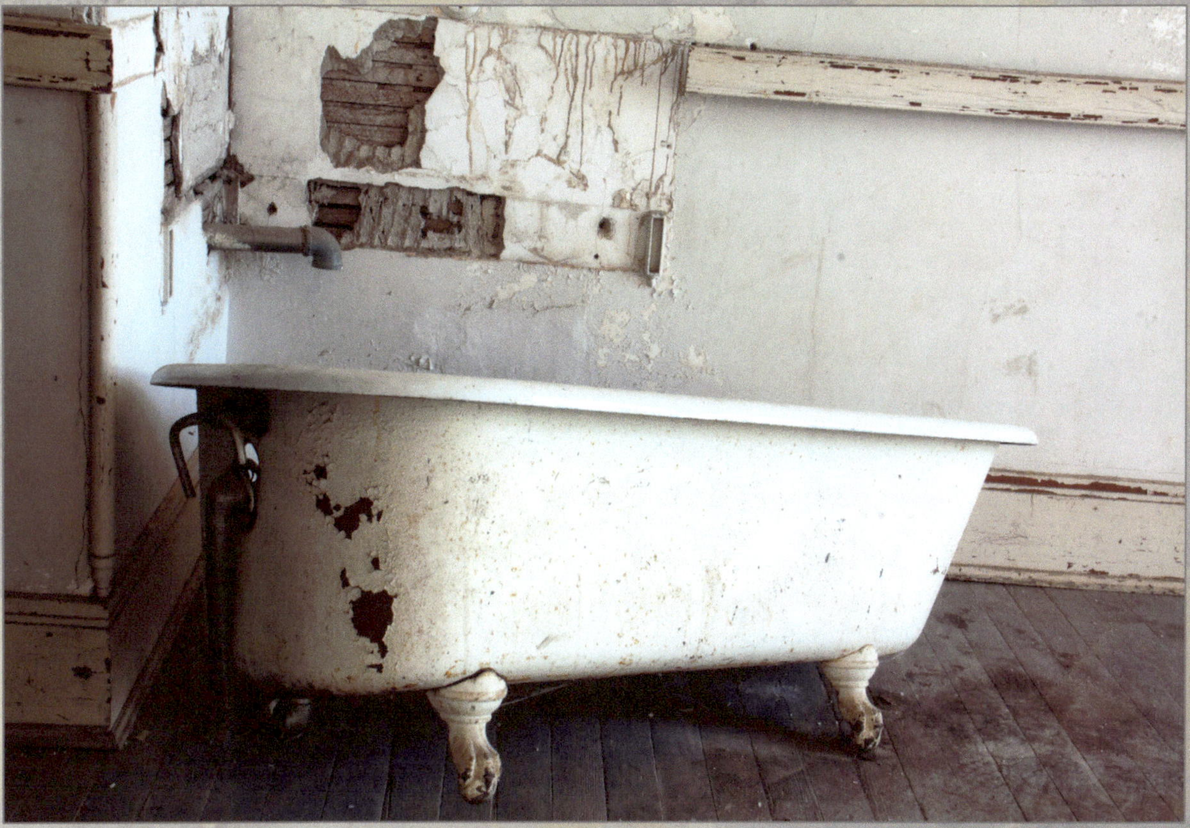

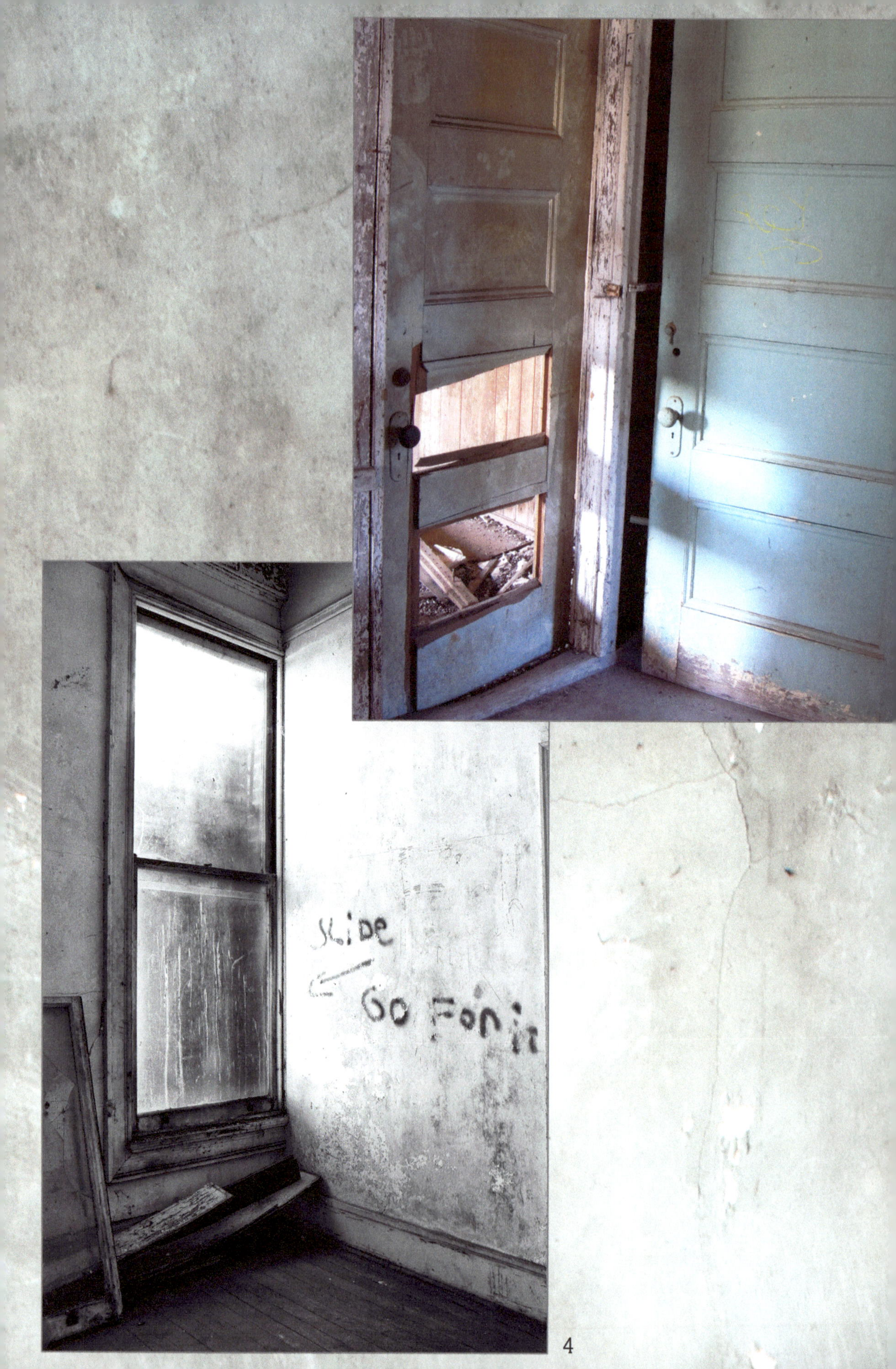
Slide
Go Fon it

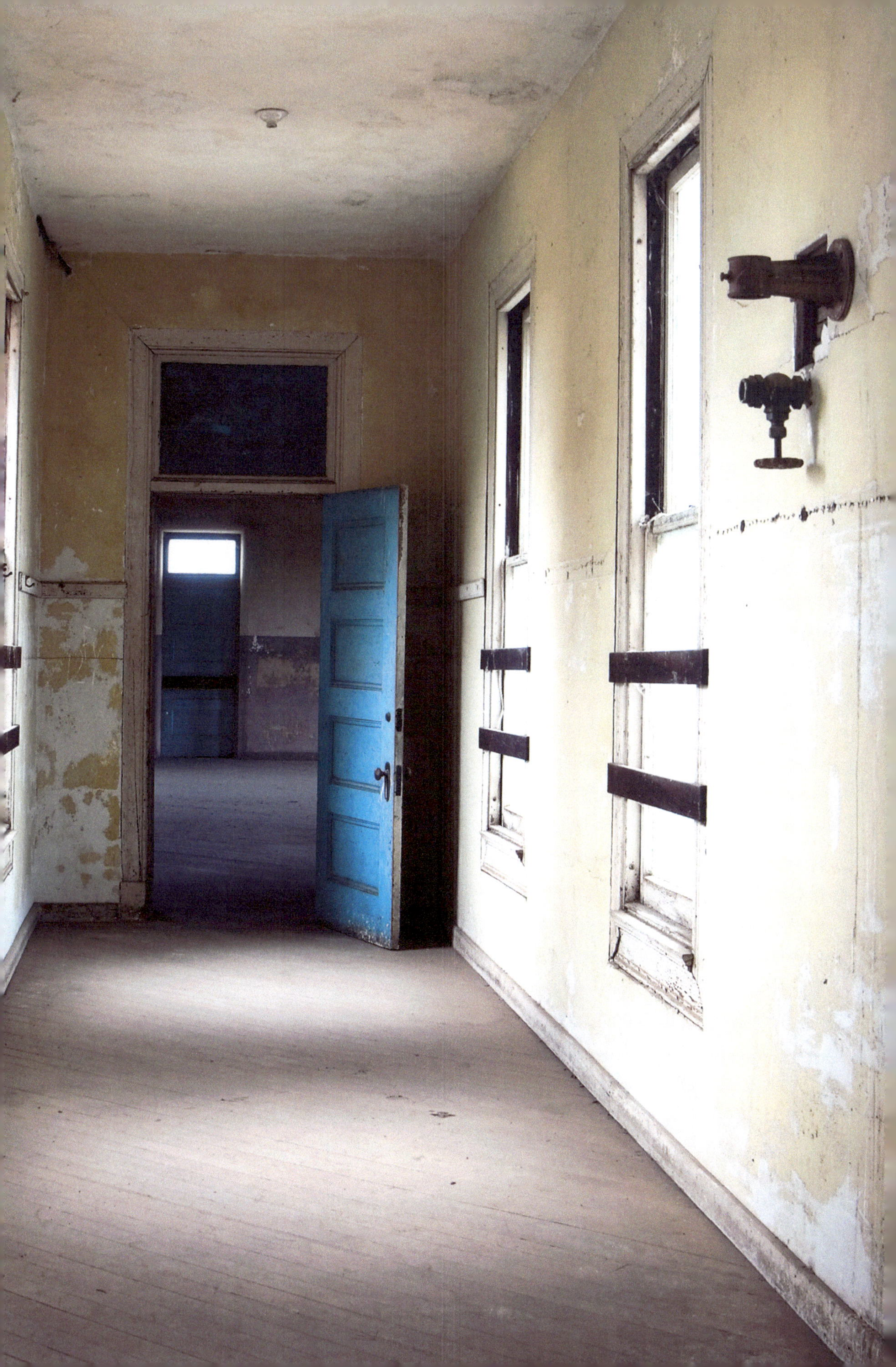

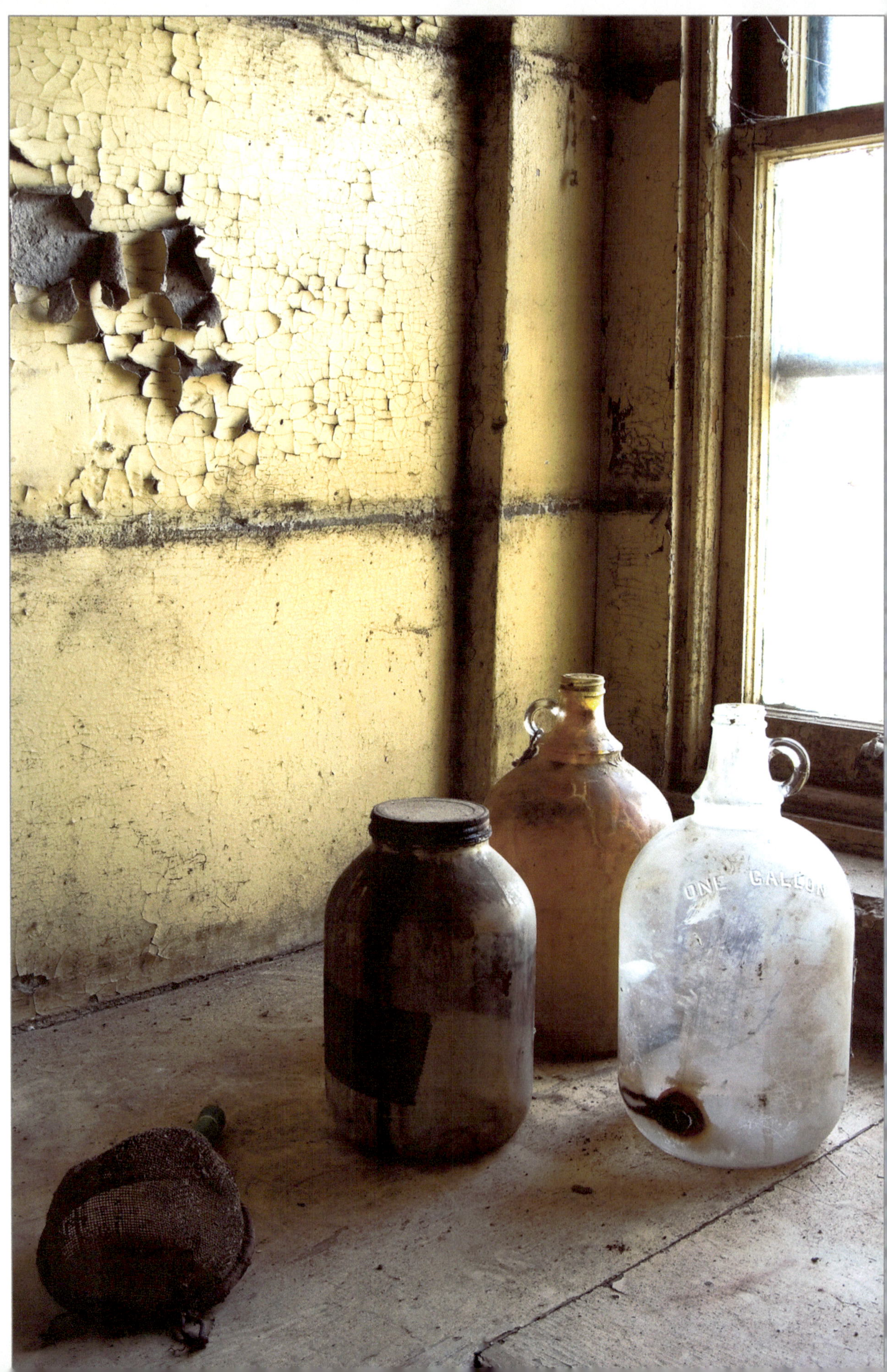

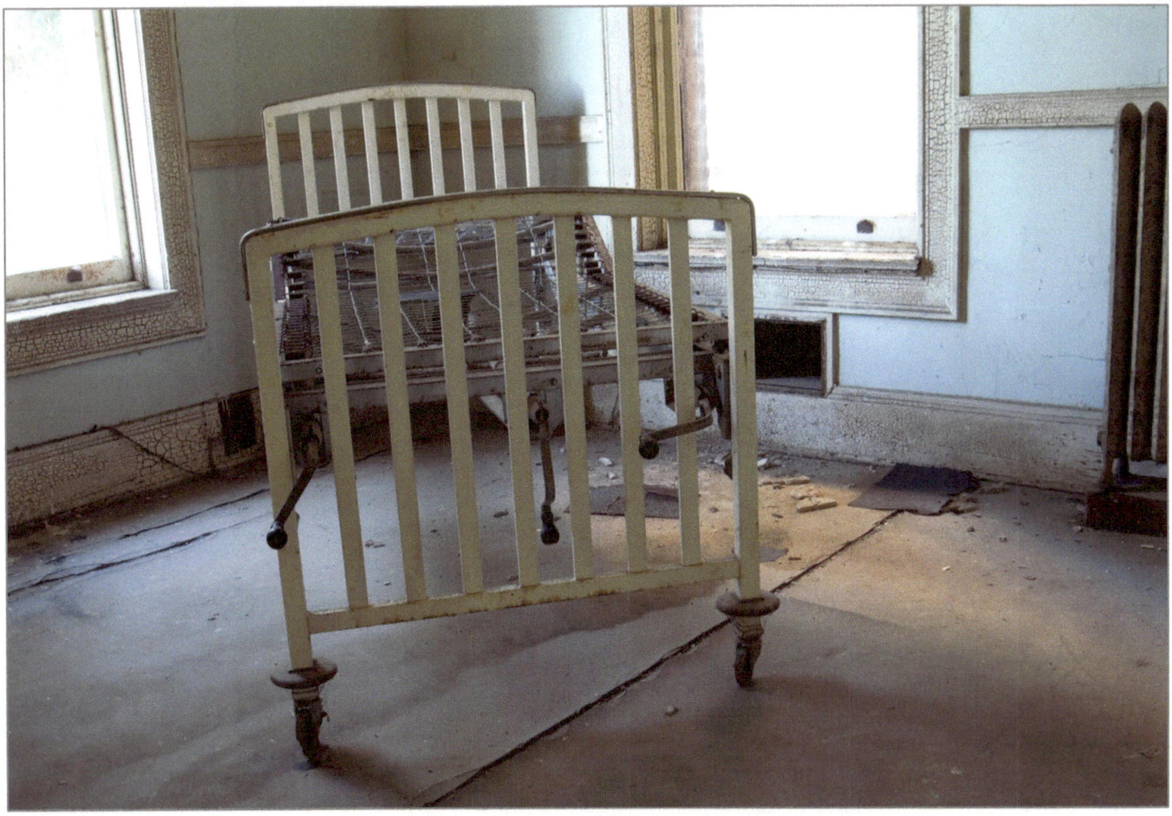

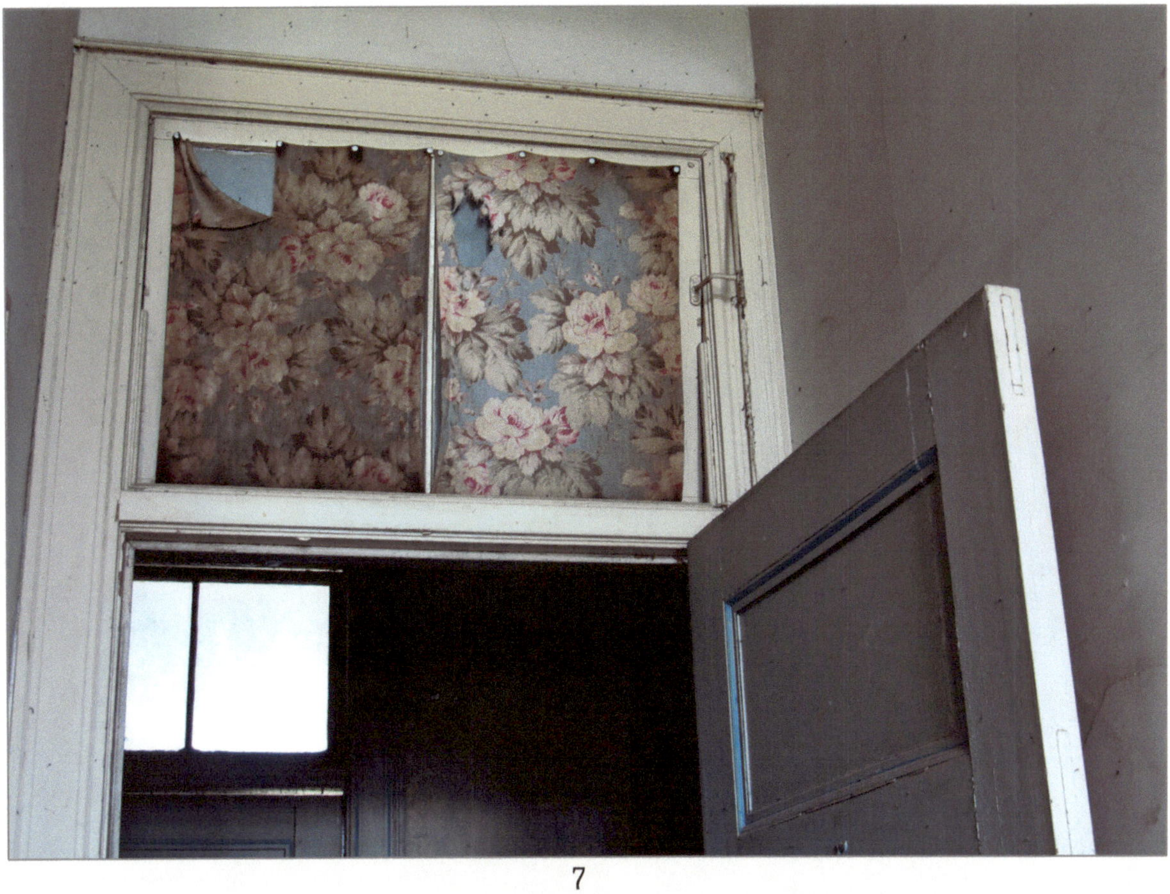

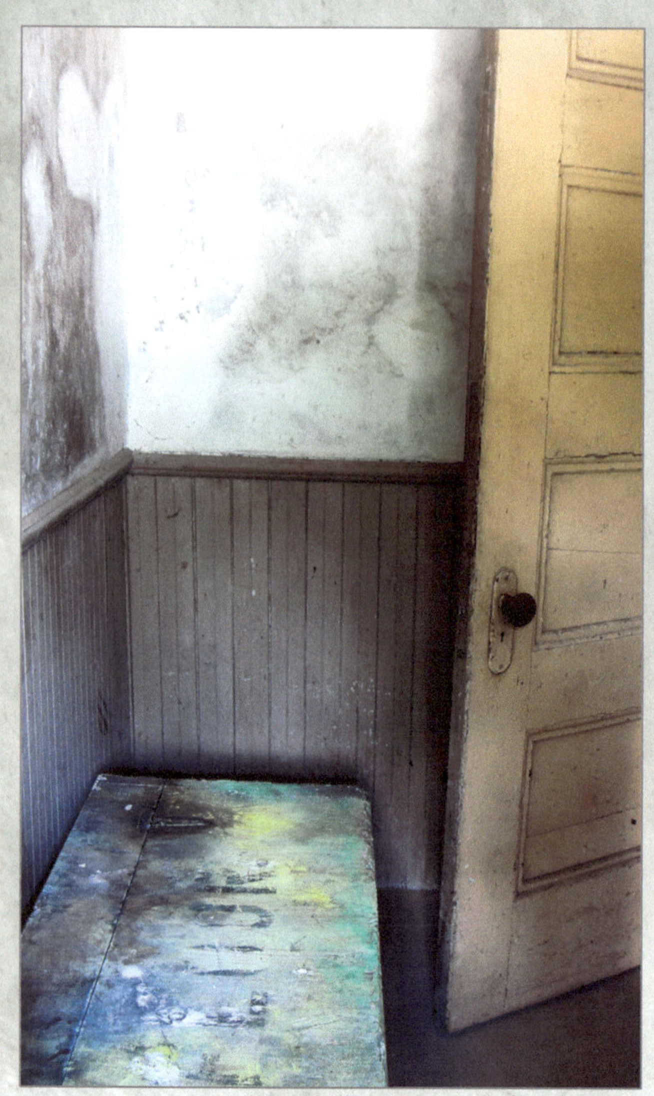

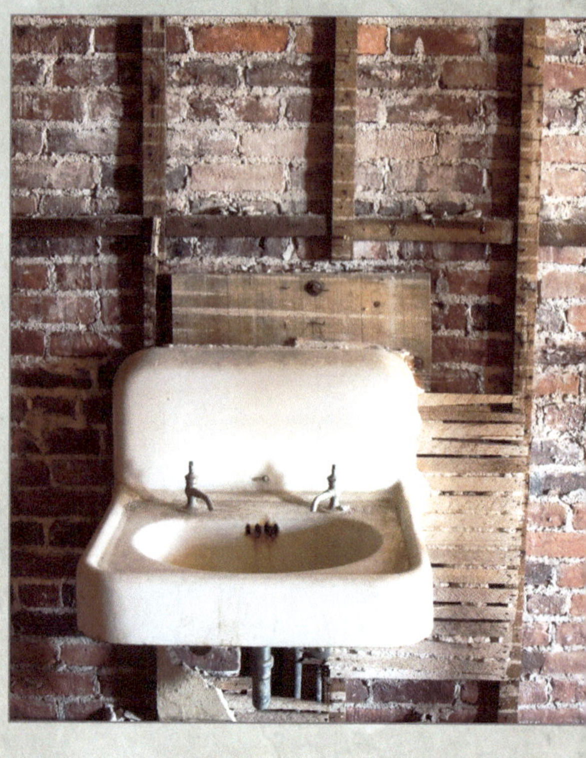

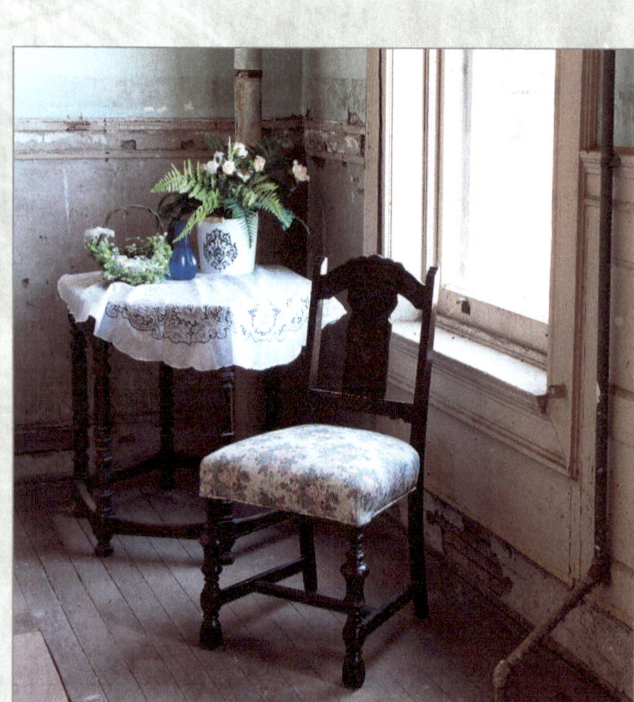

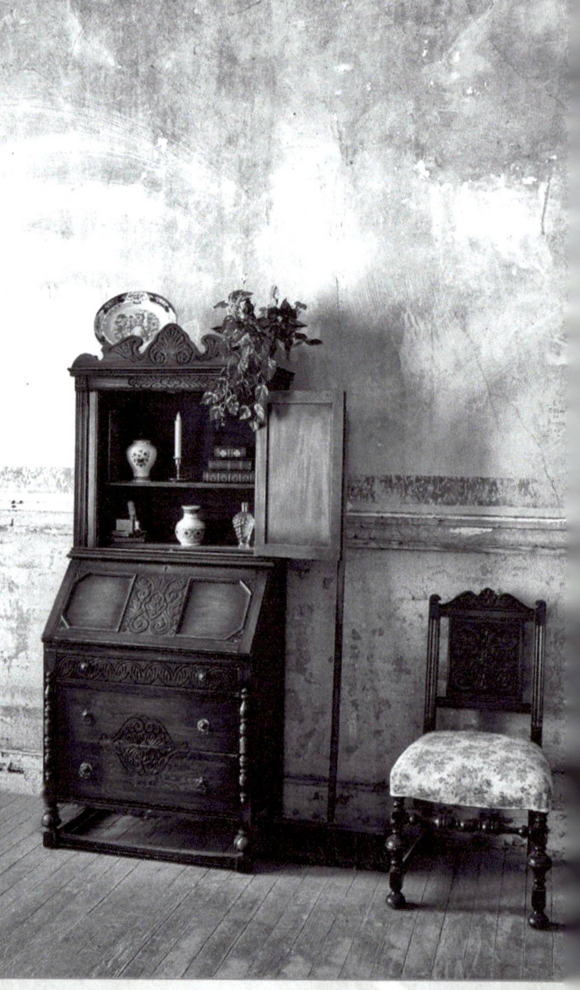

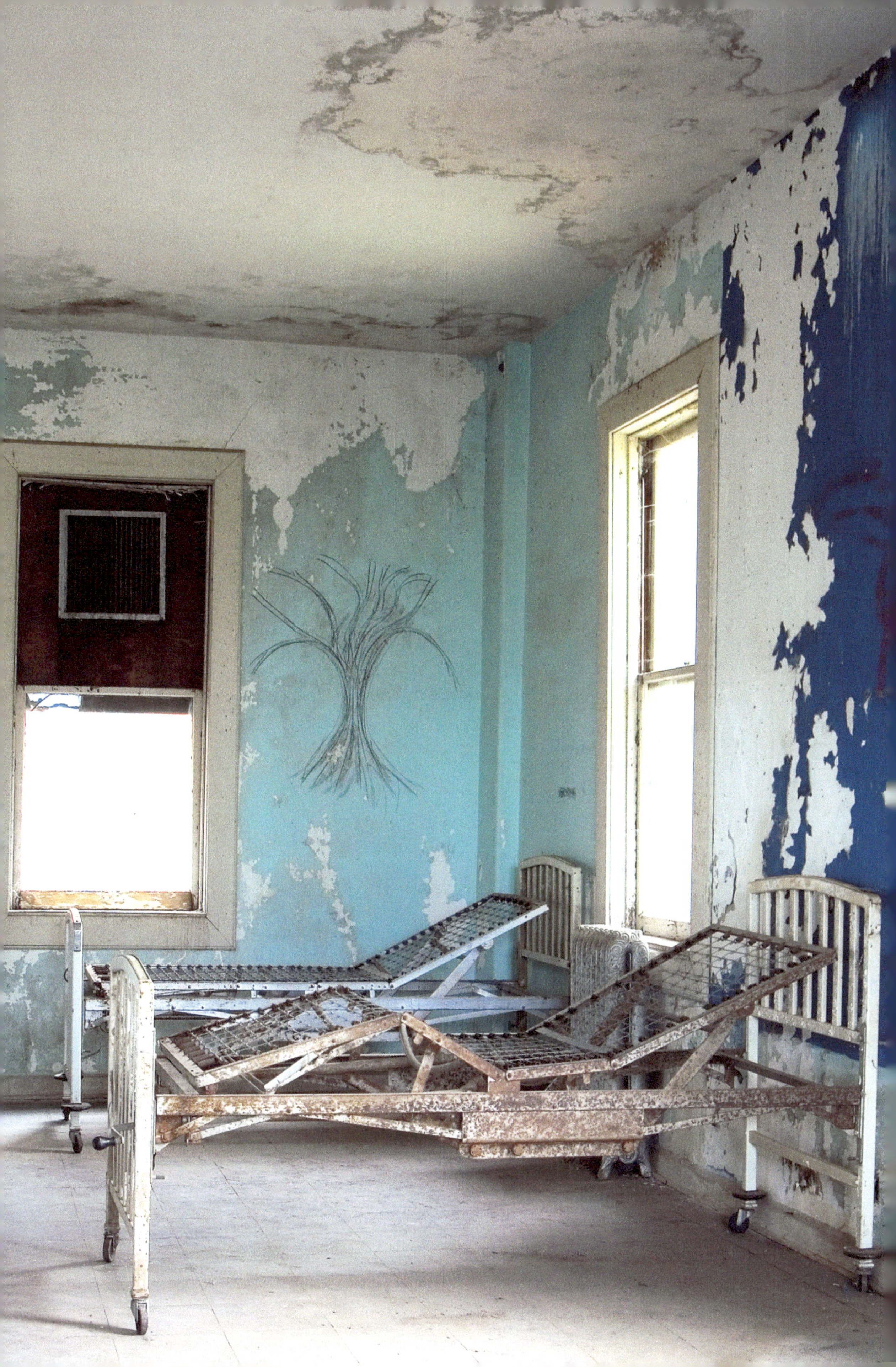

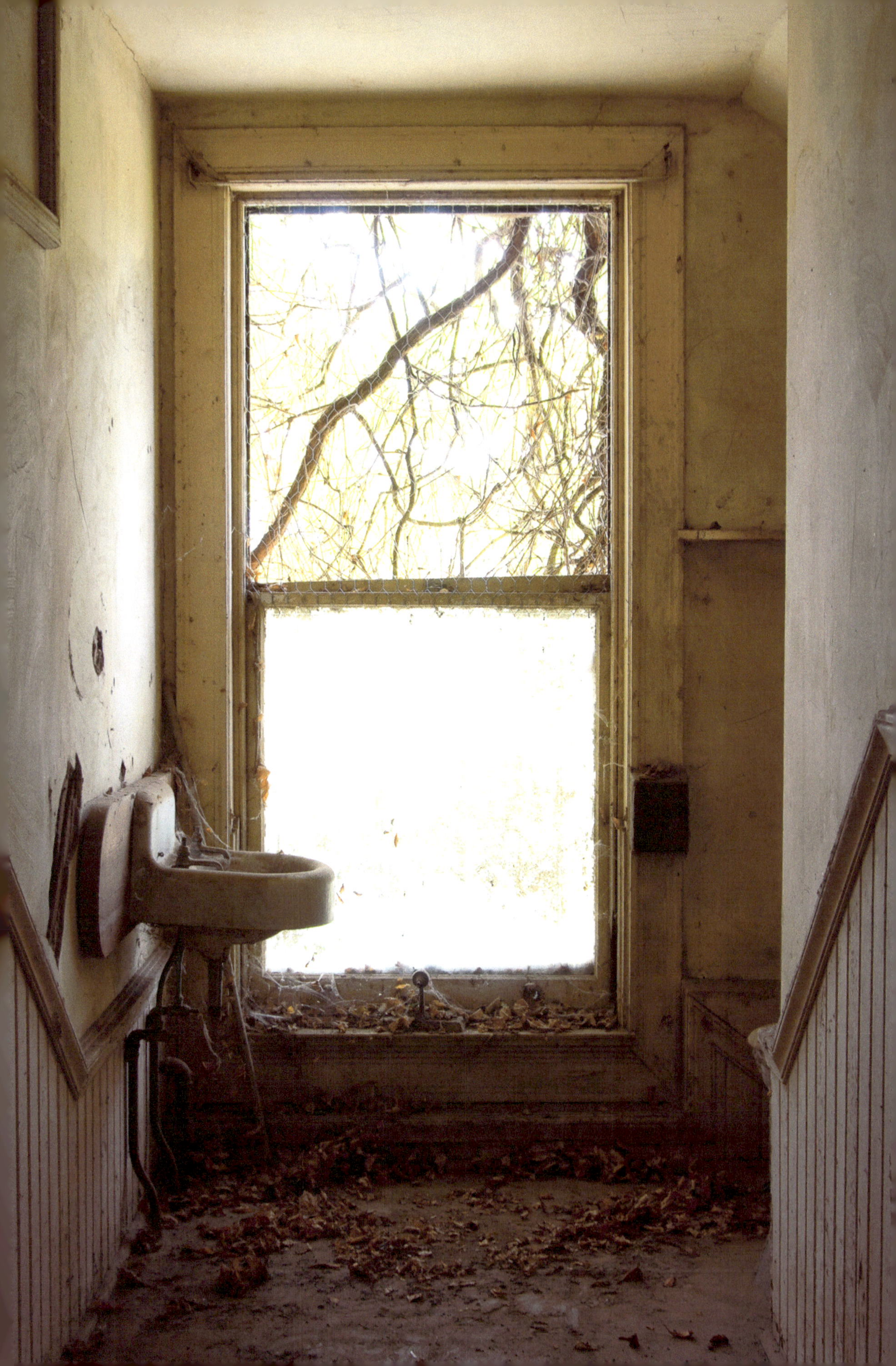

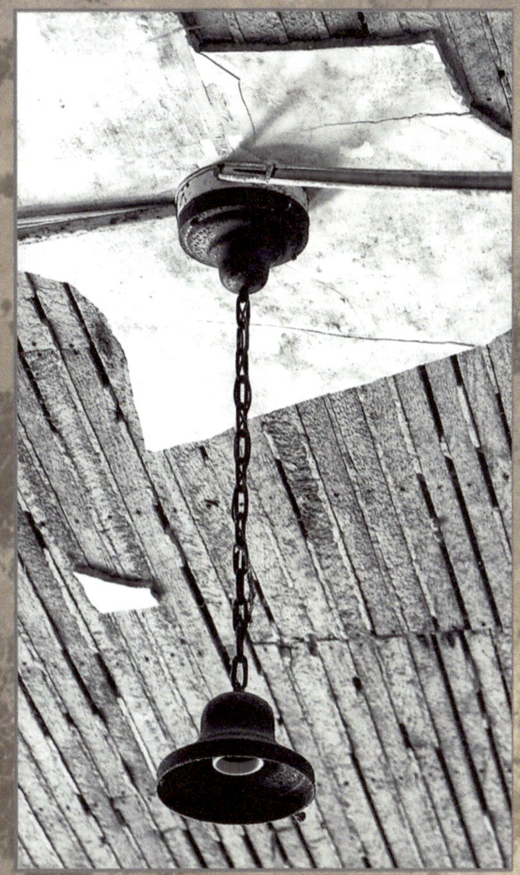

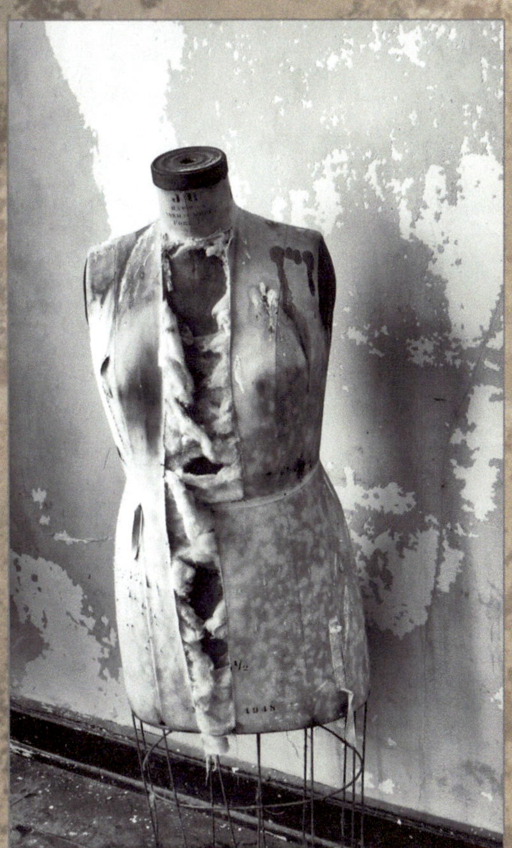

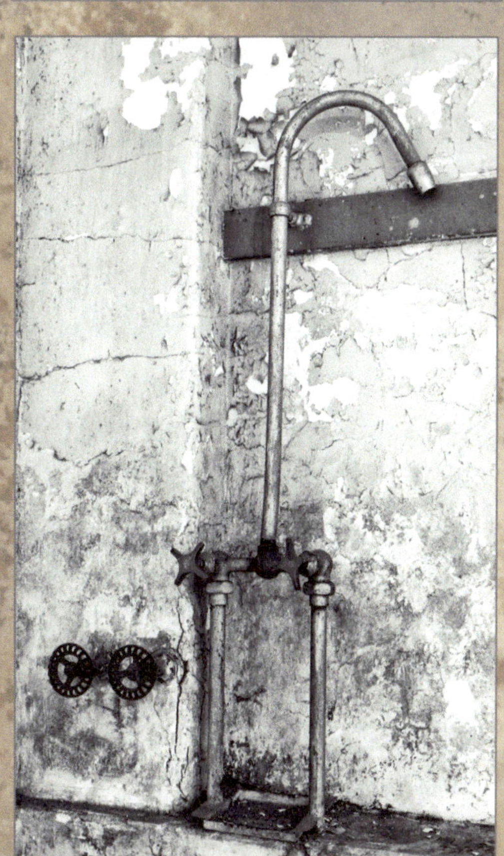

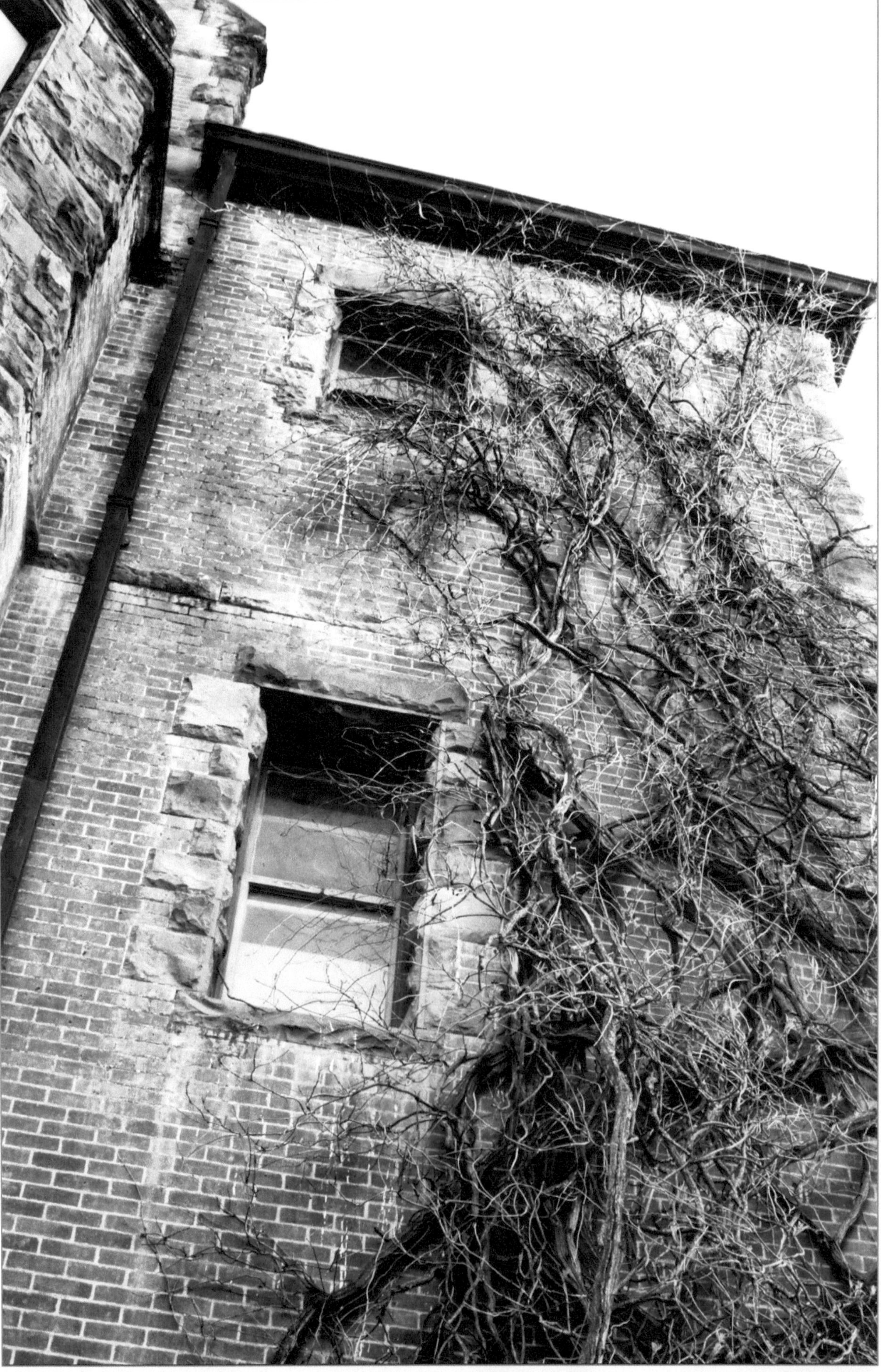

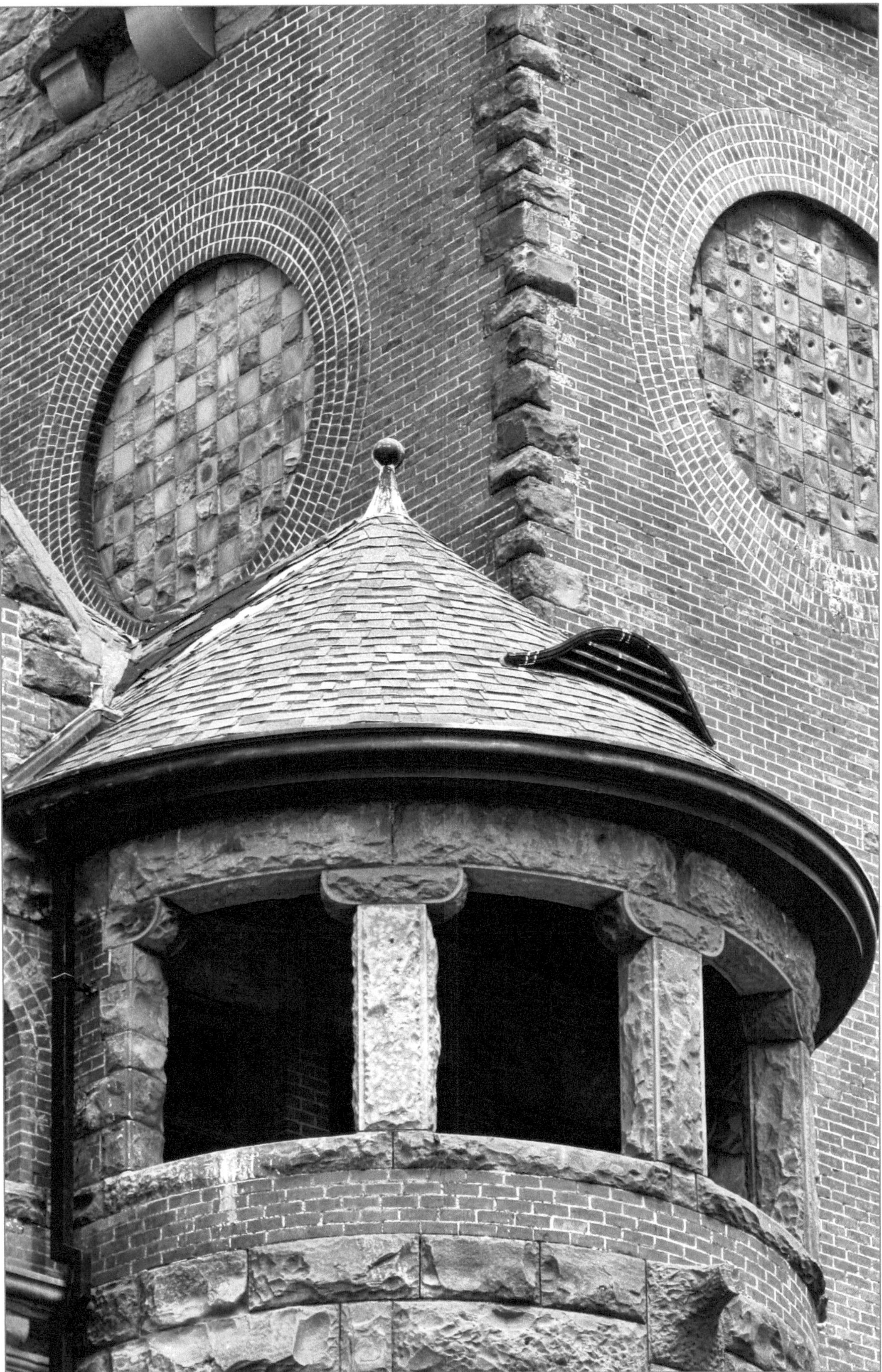

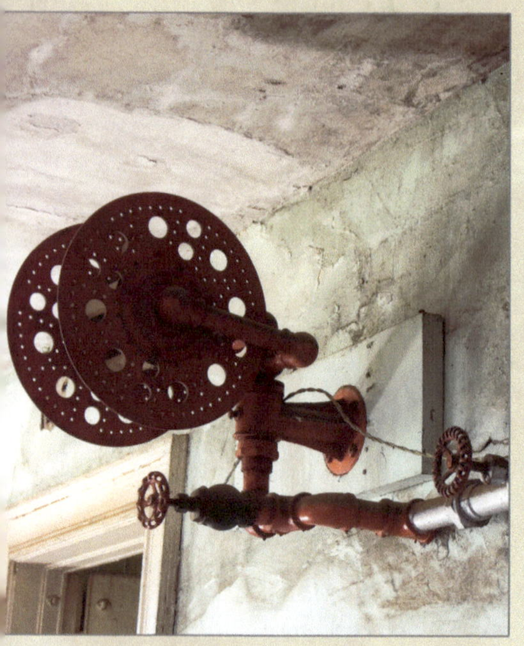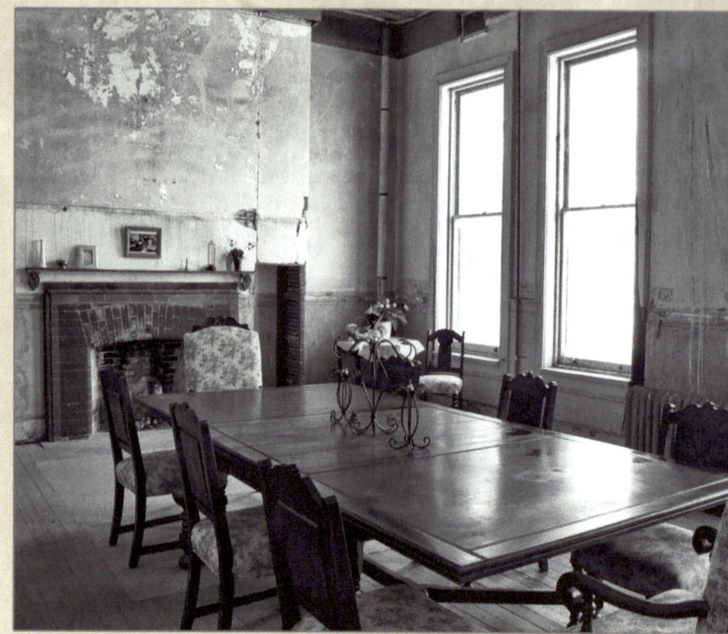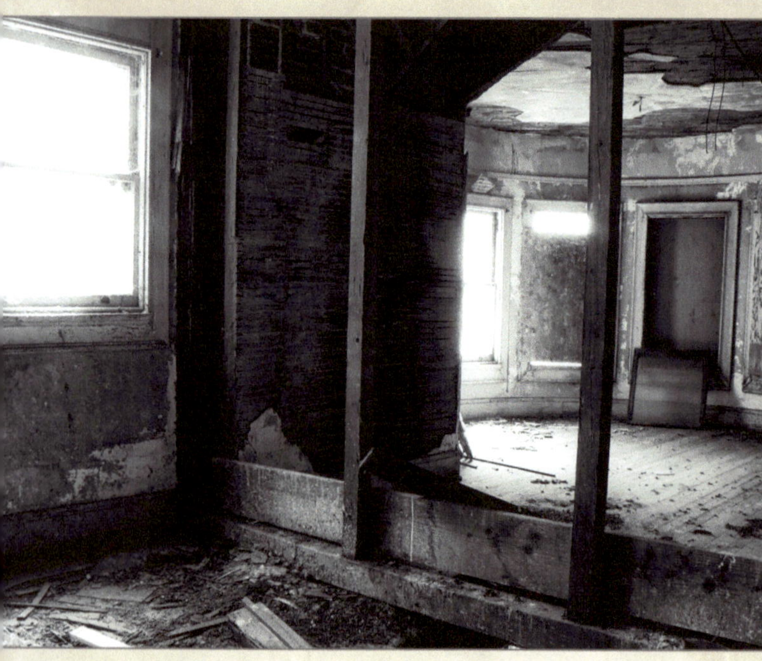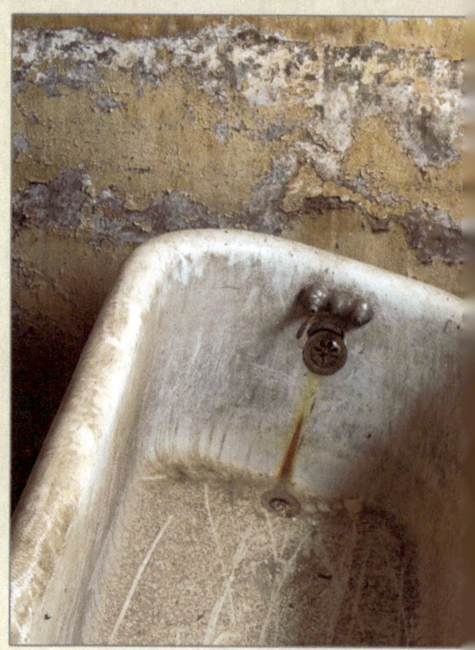

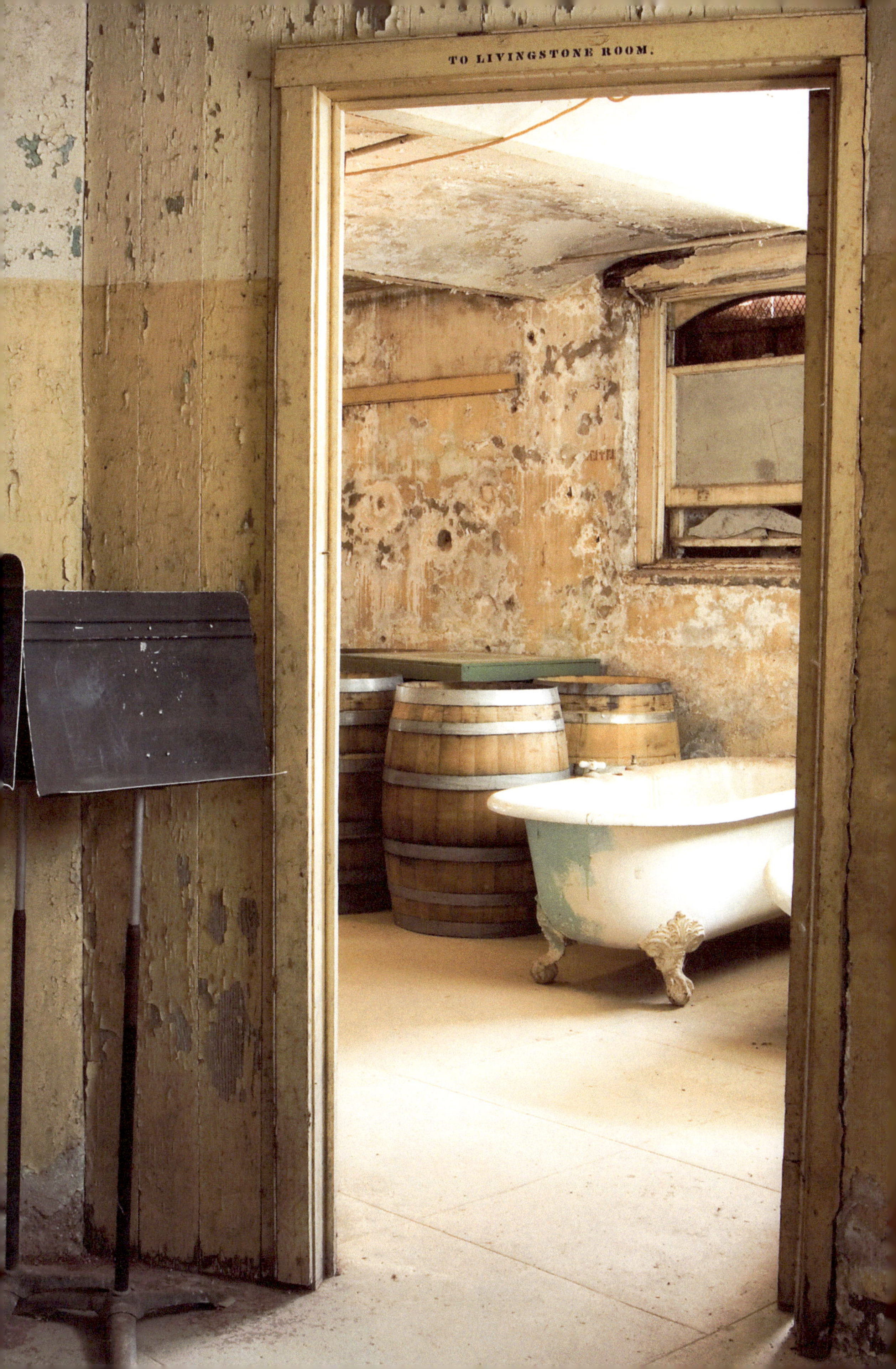

TO LIVINGSTONE ROOM.

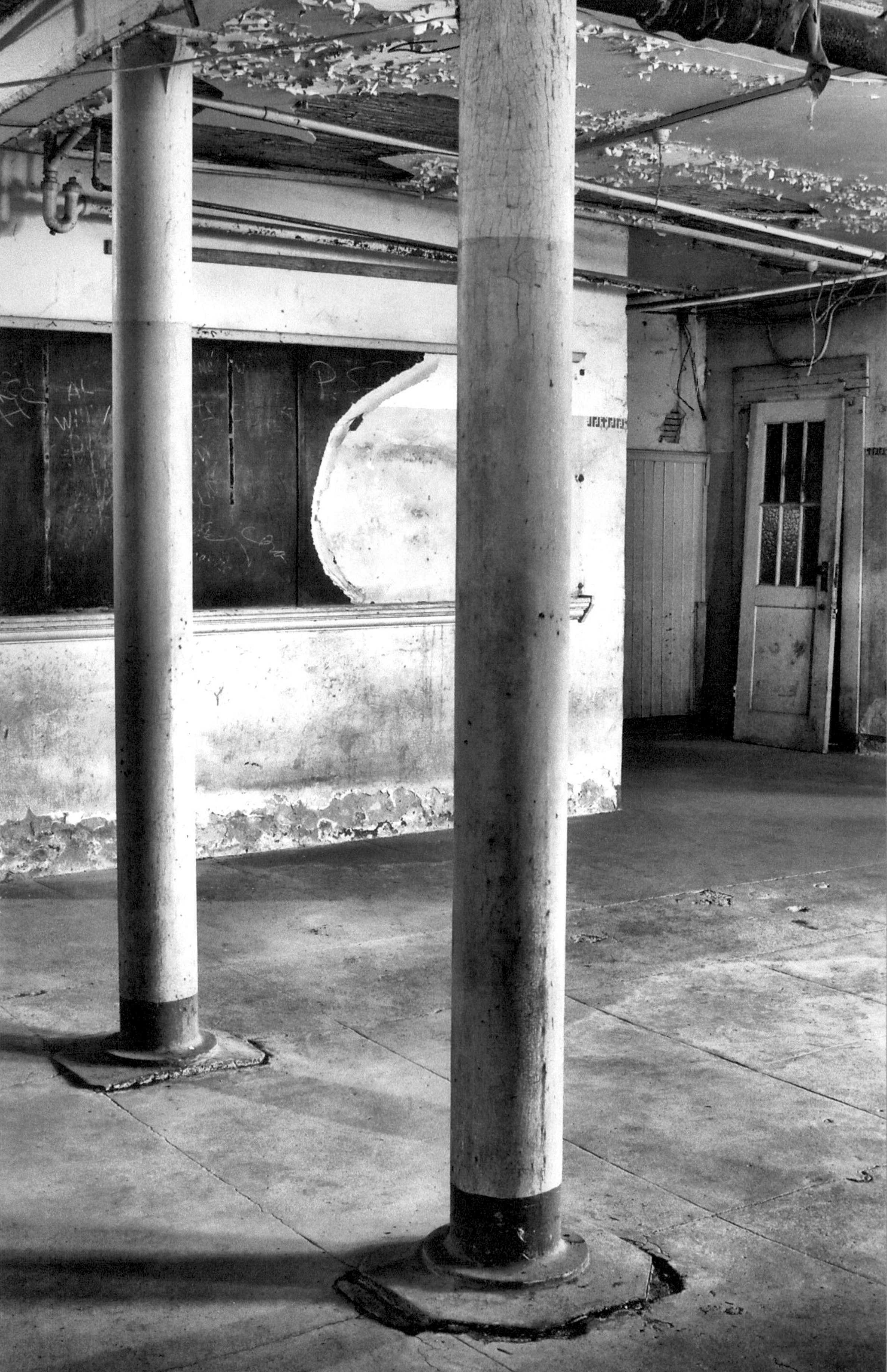

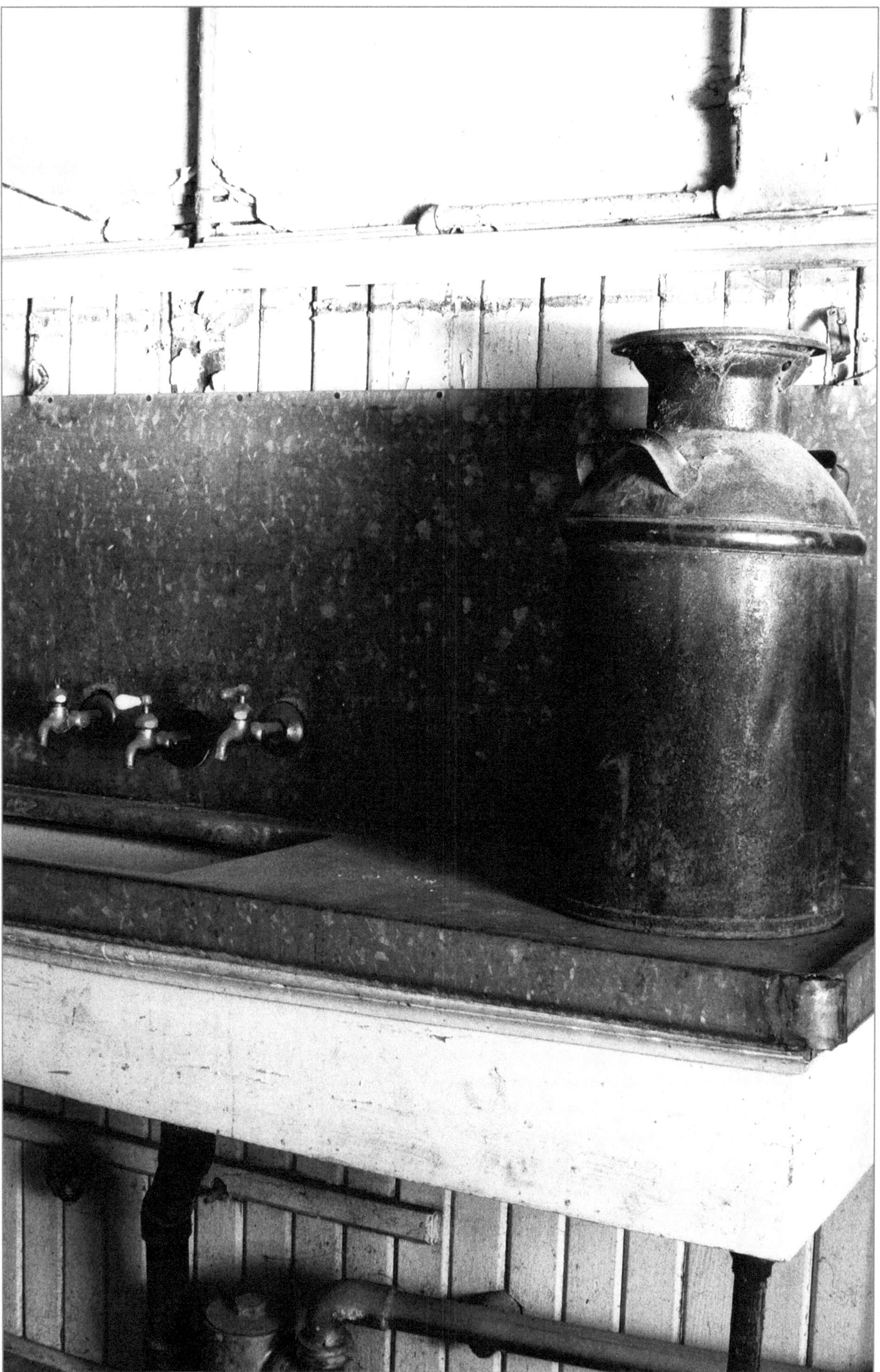

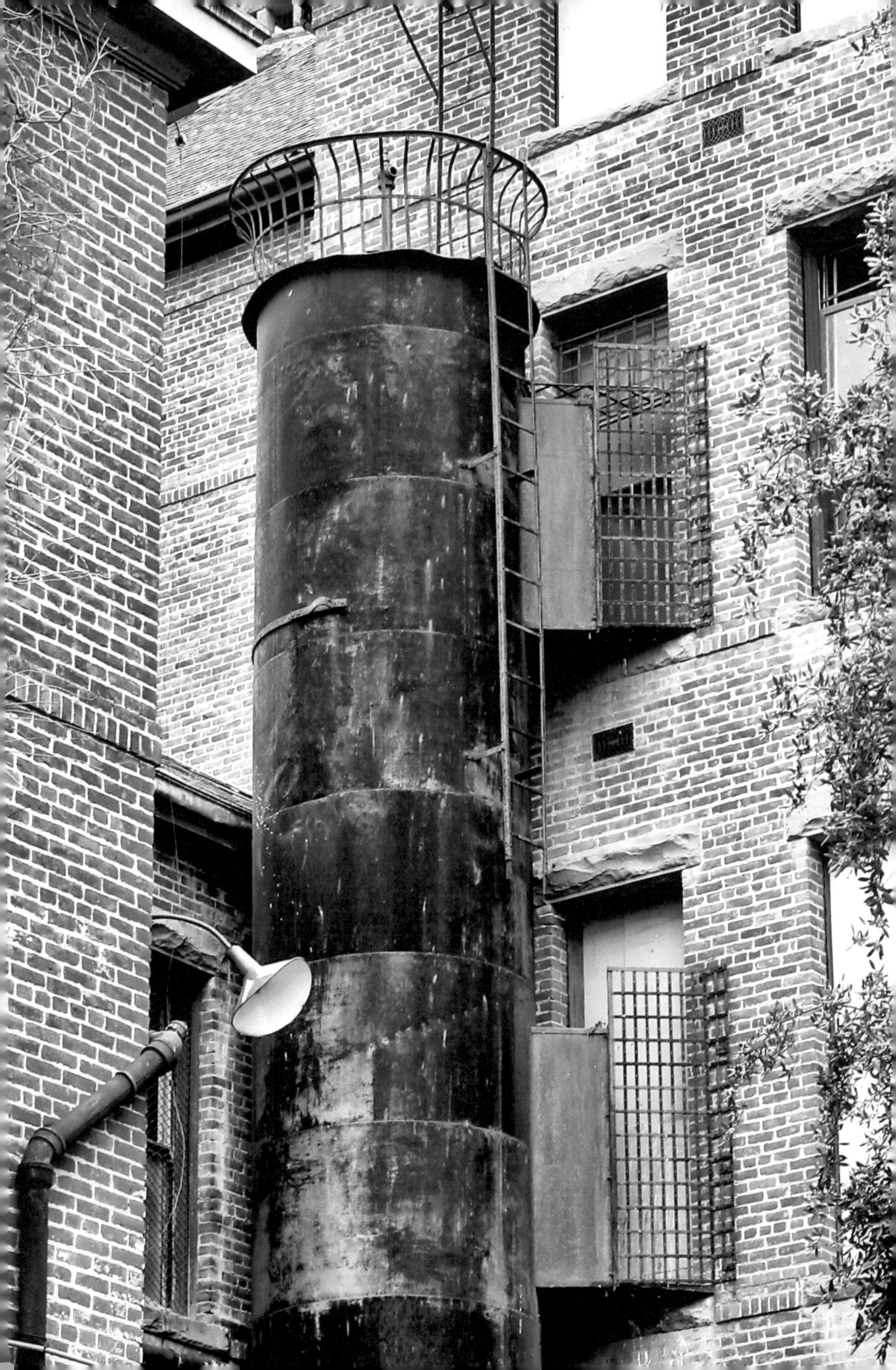

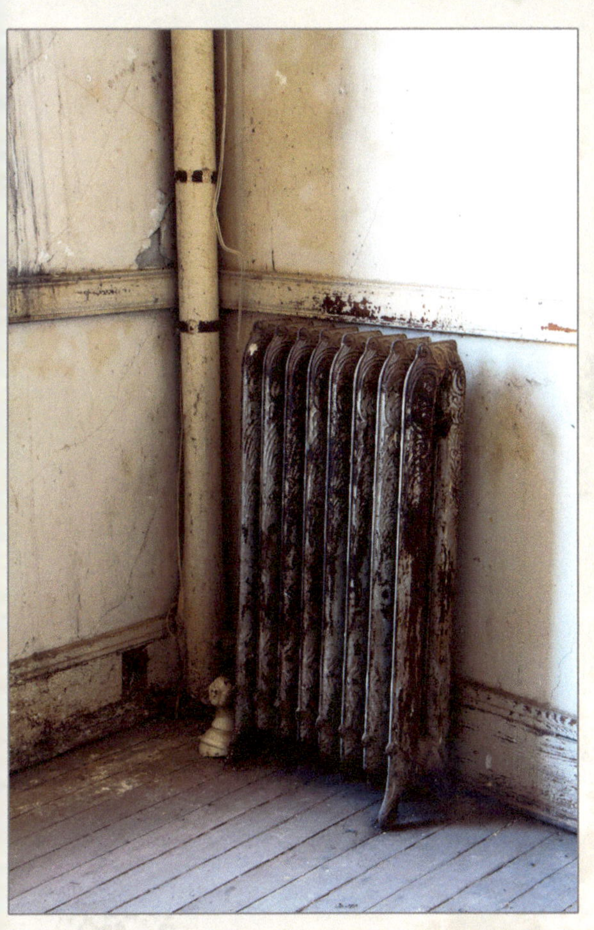
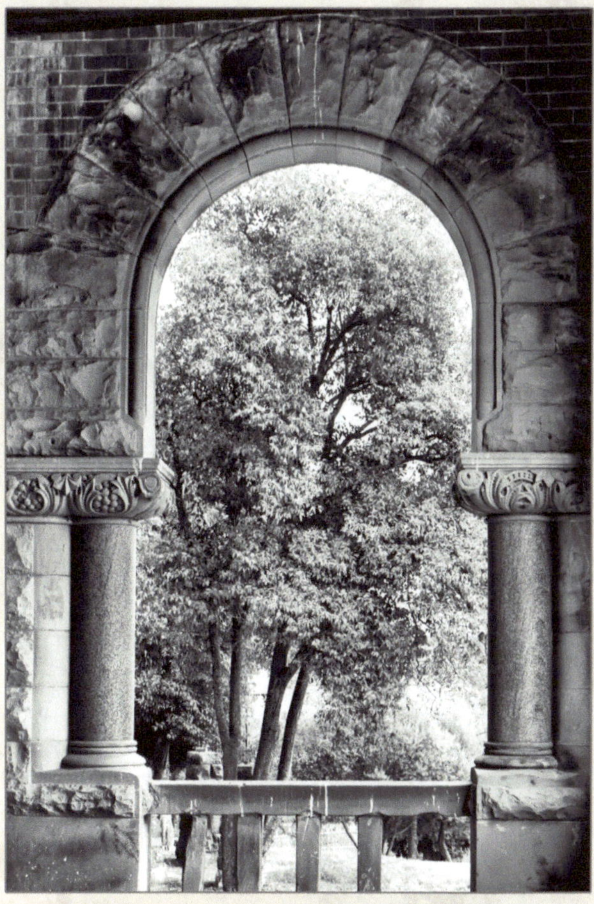

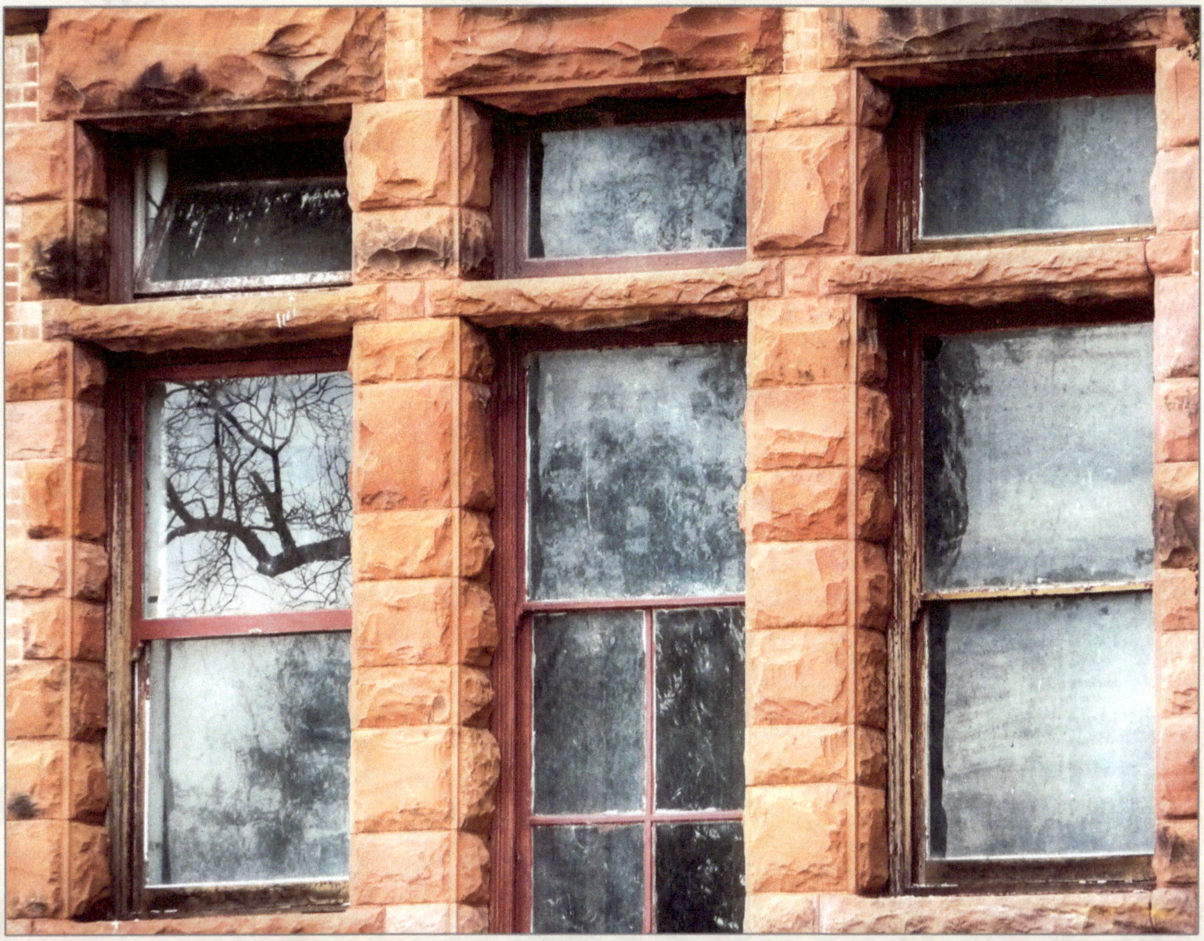

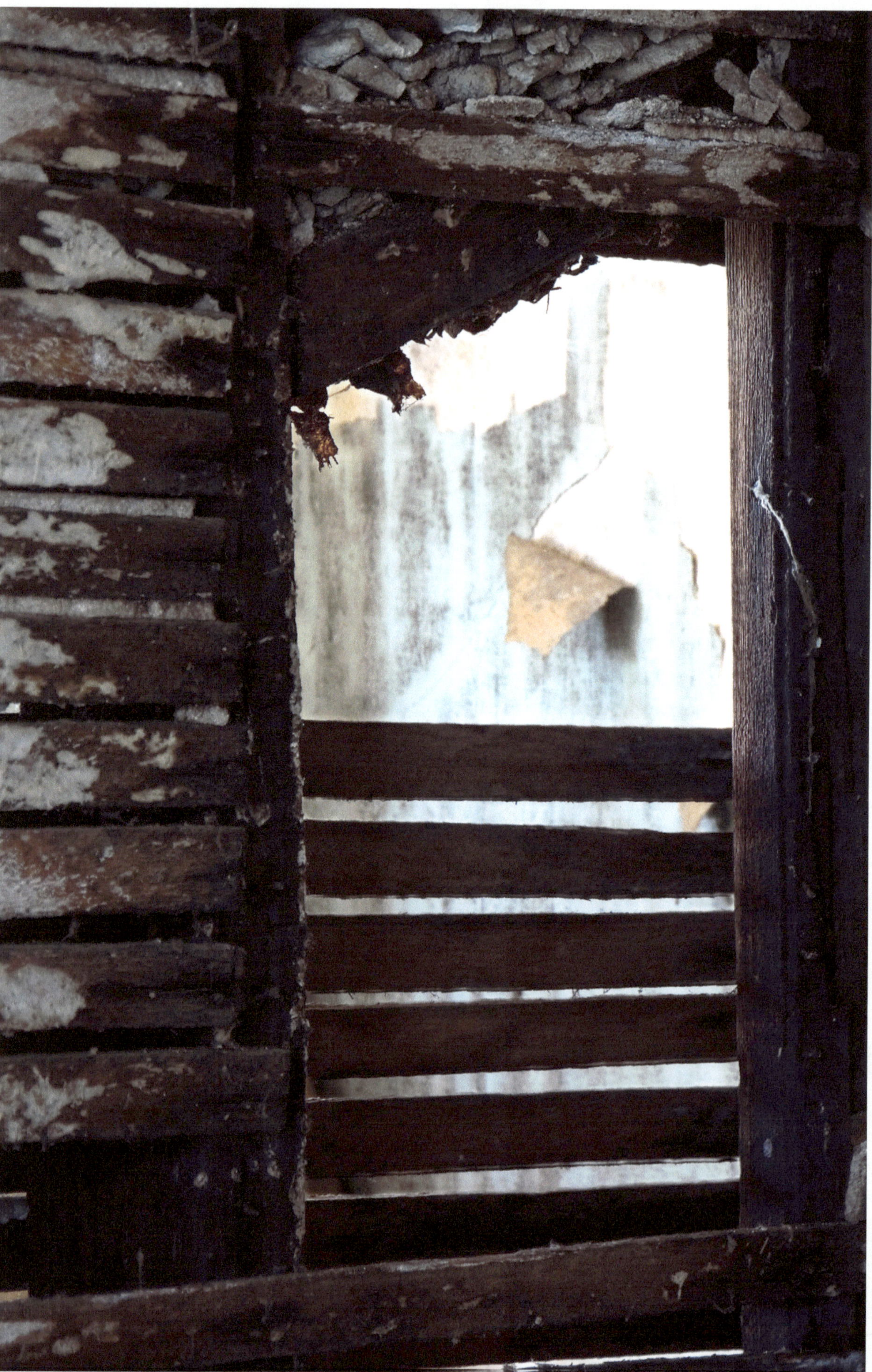

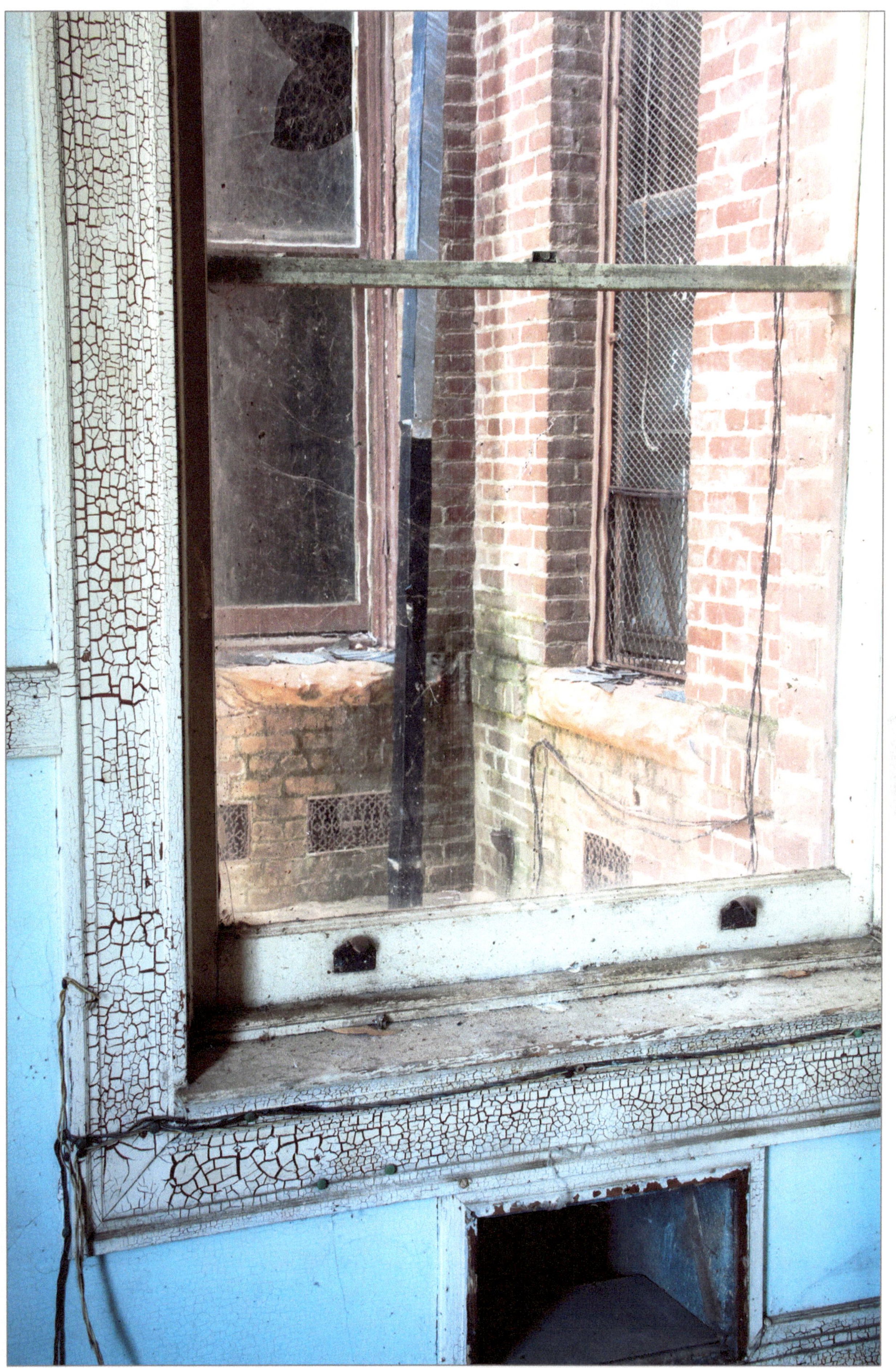

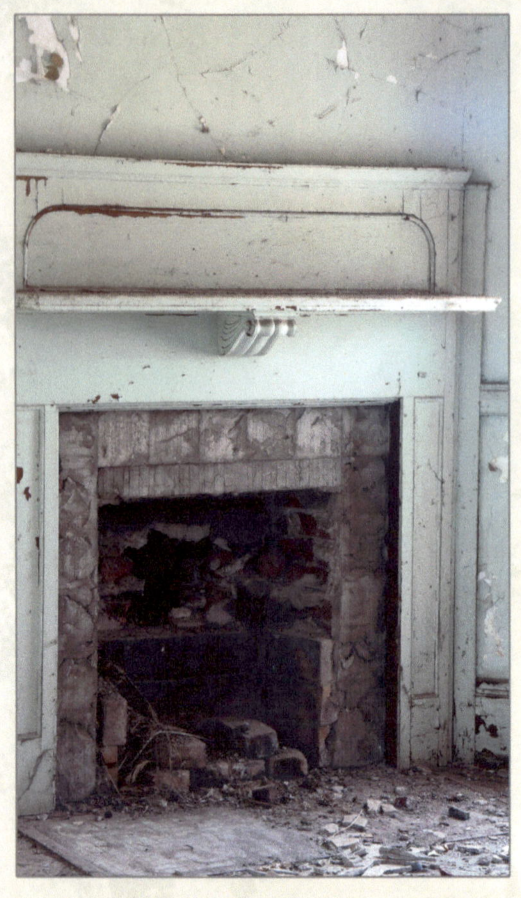

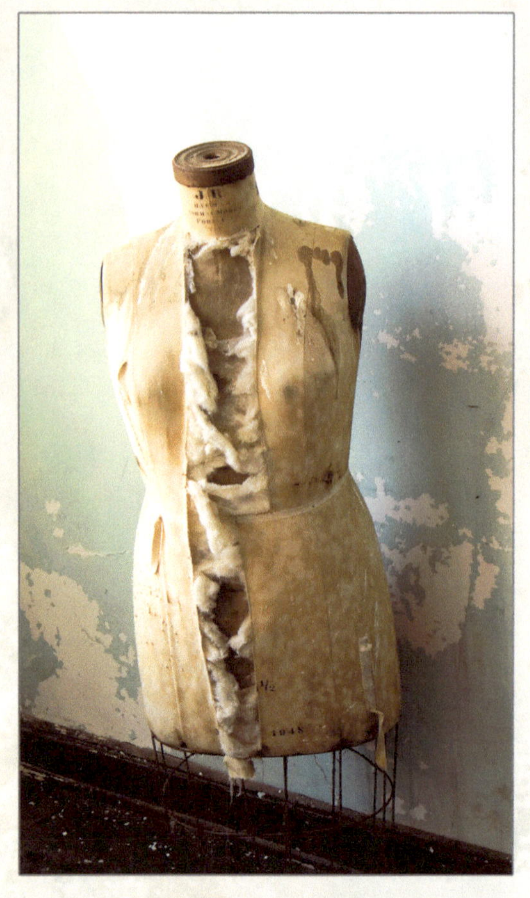

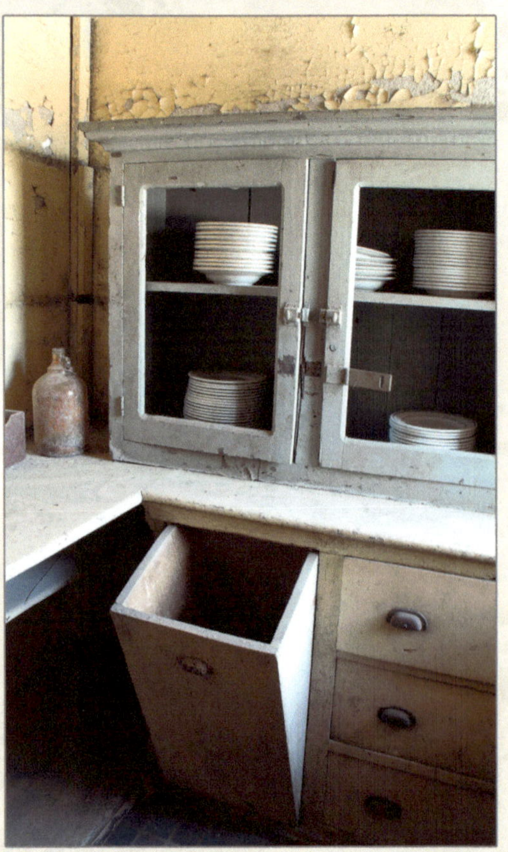

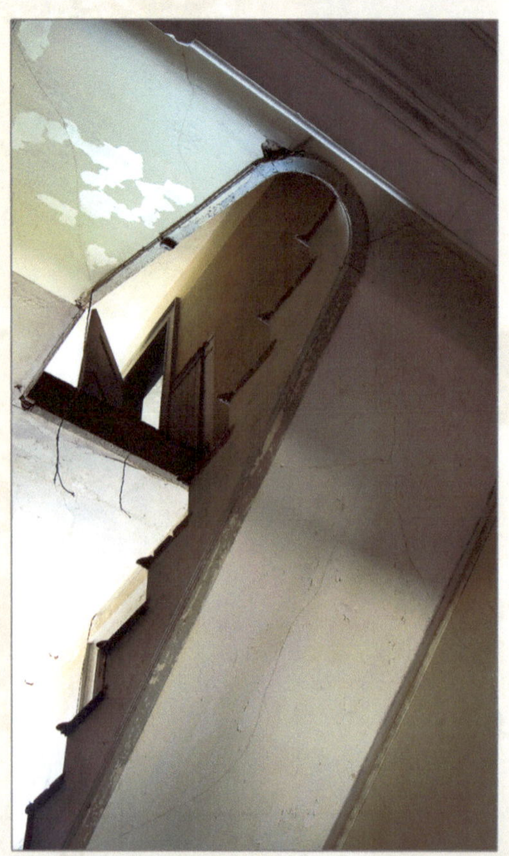

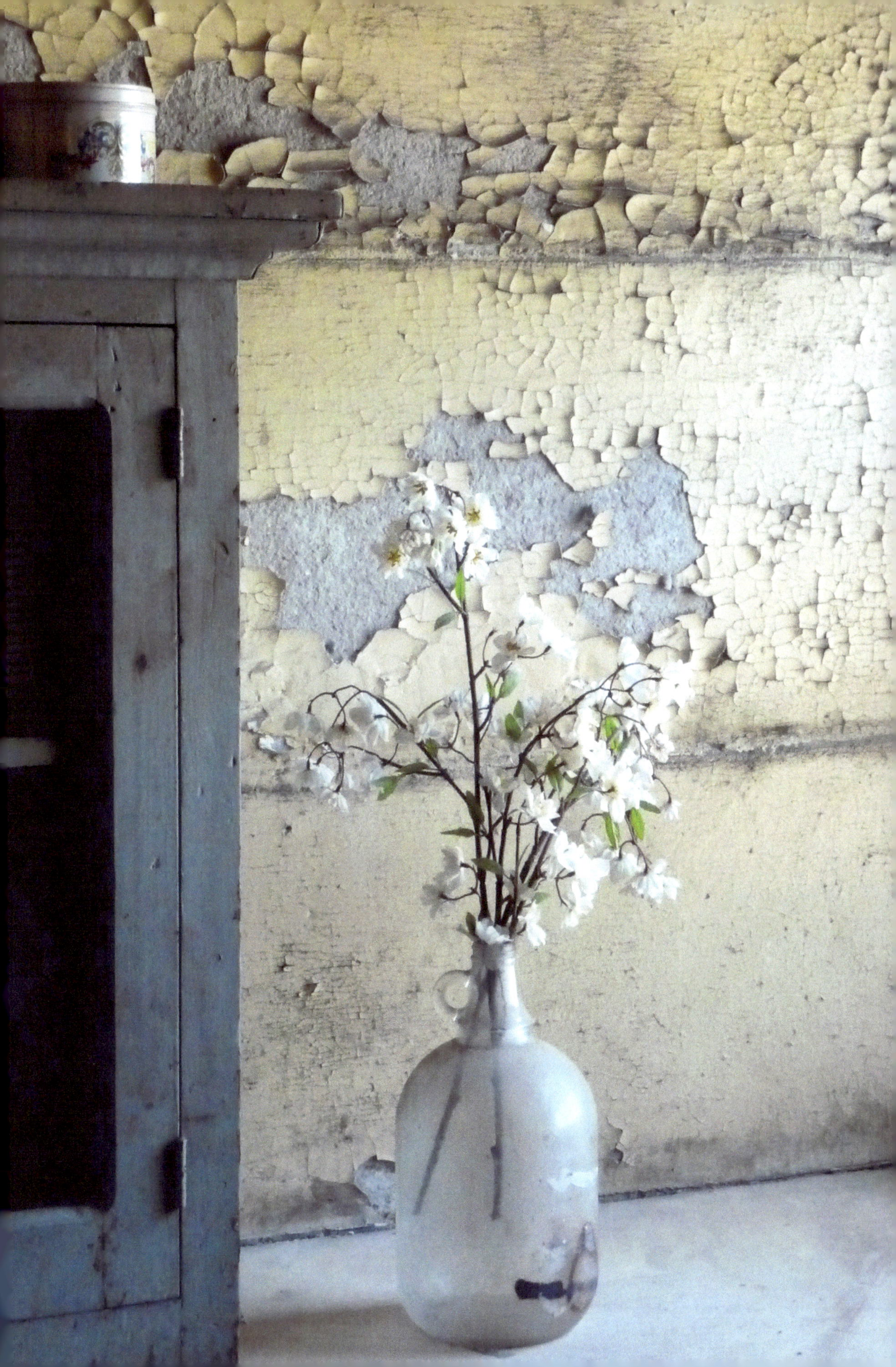

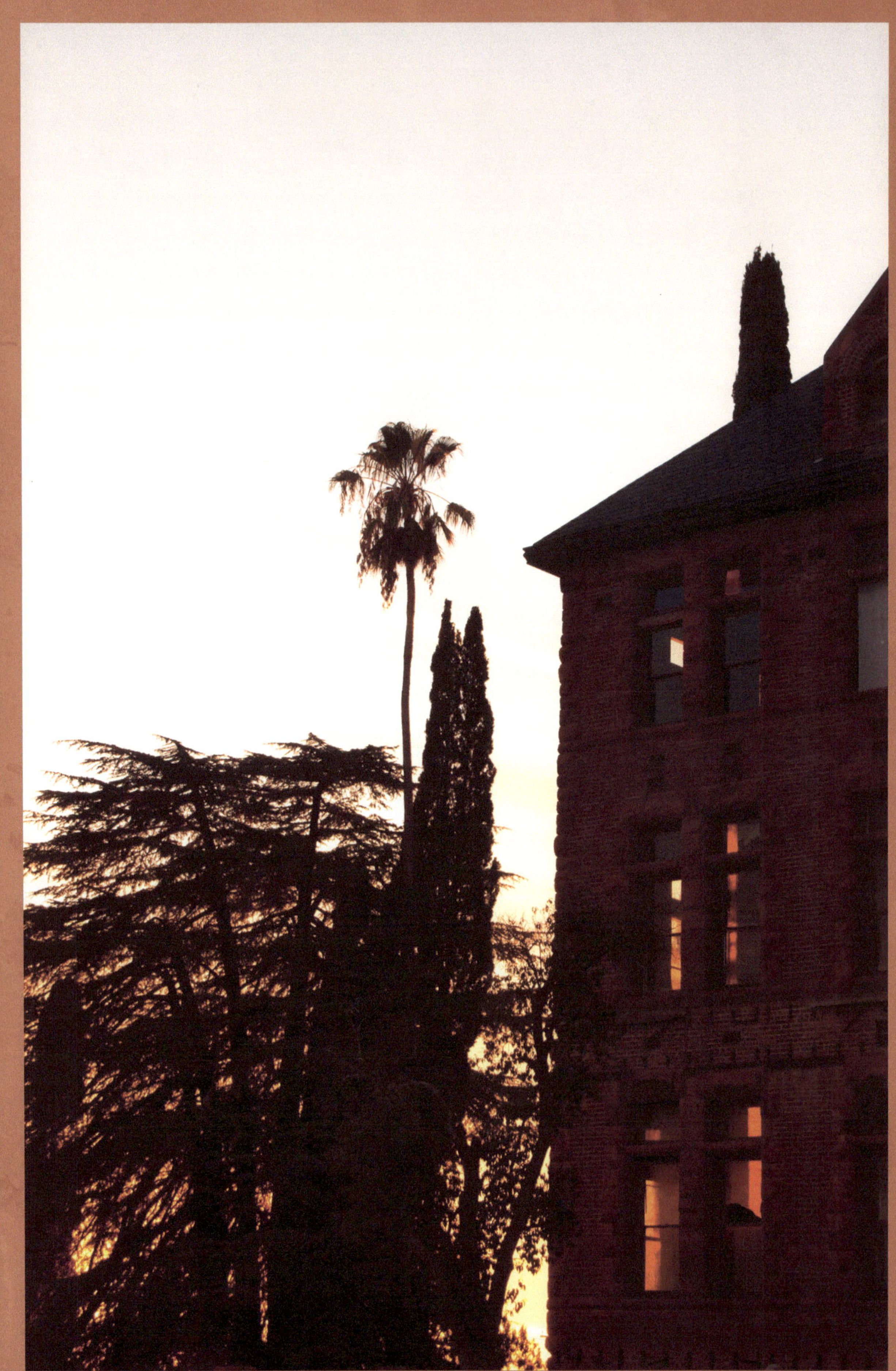

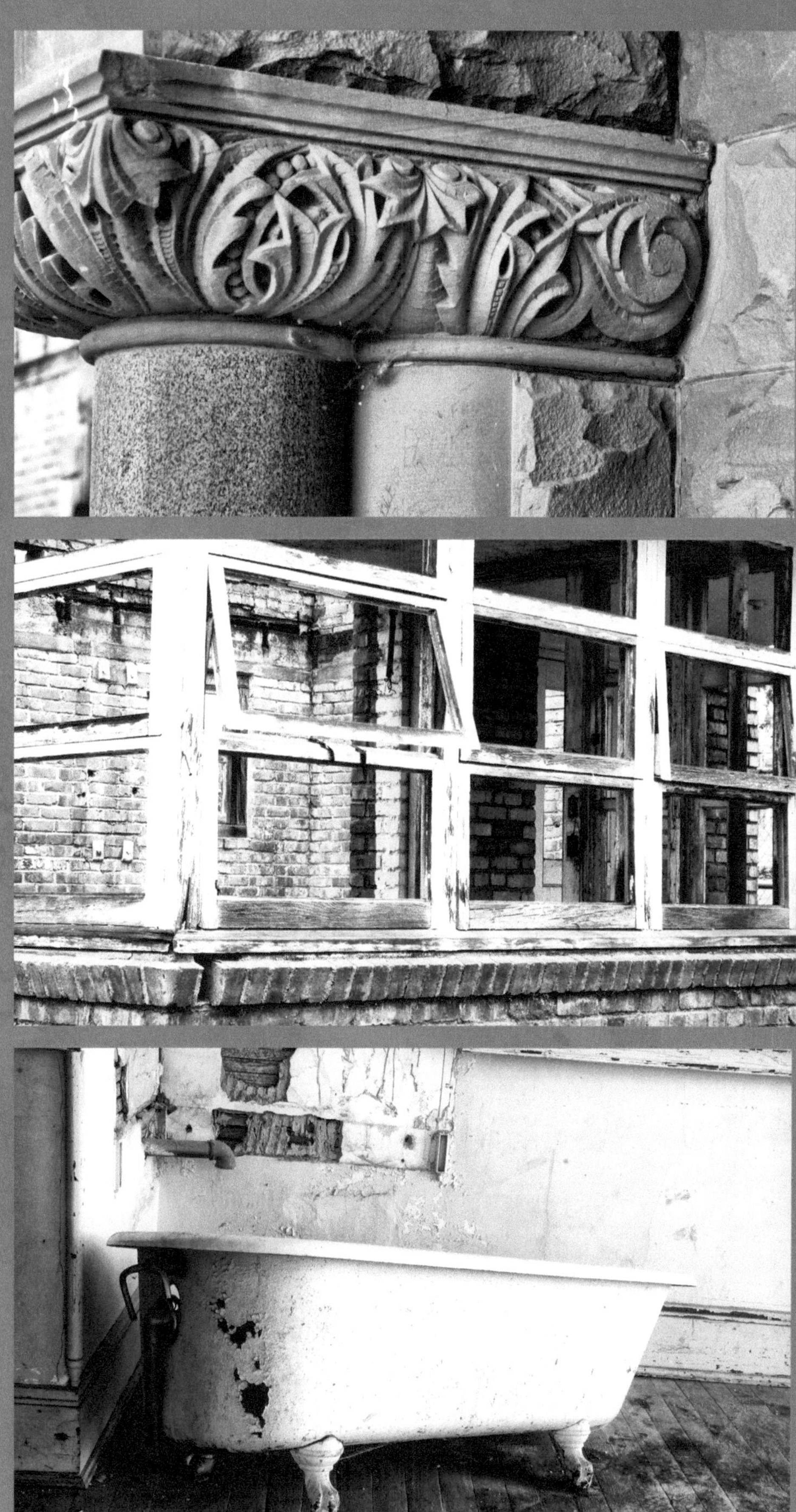

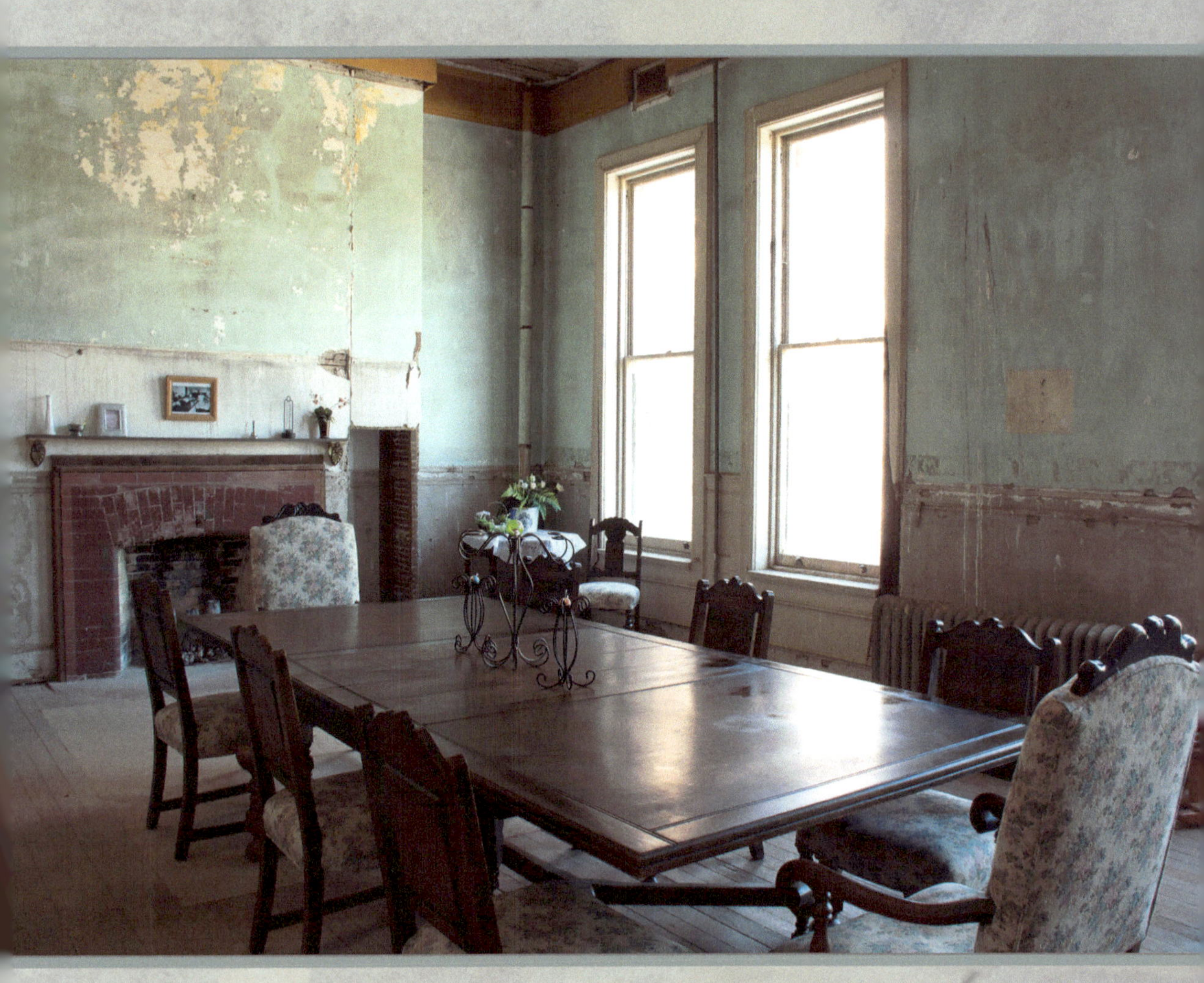

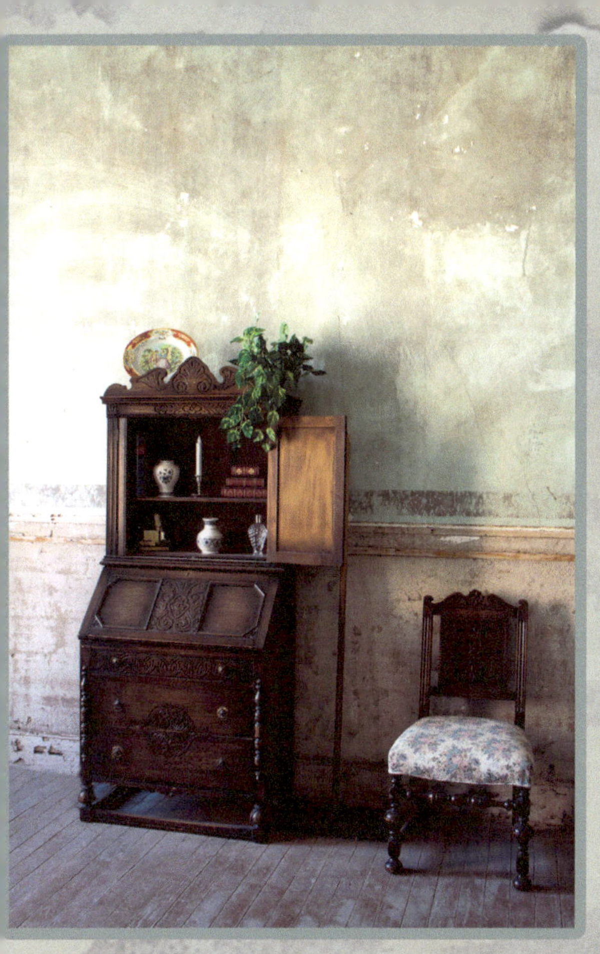
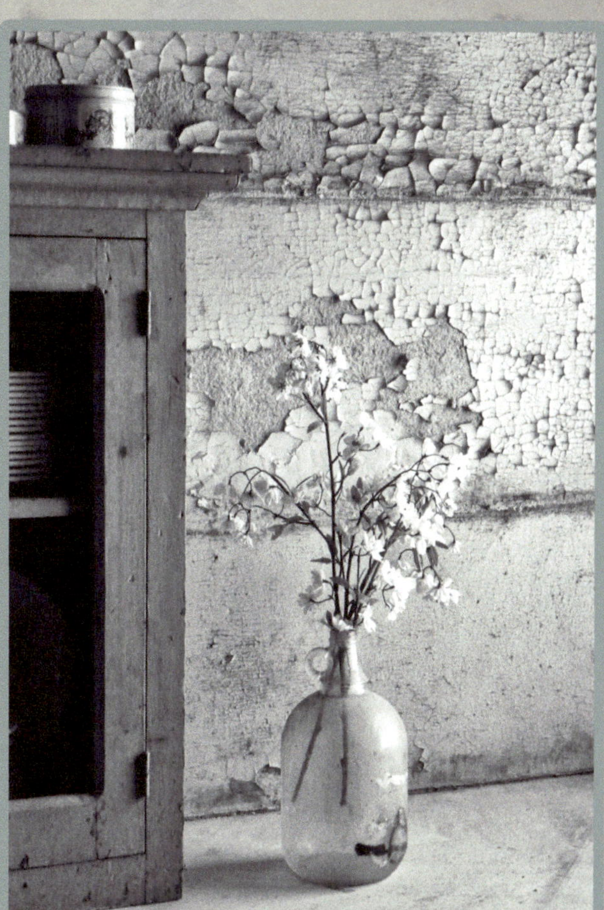

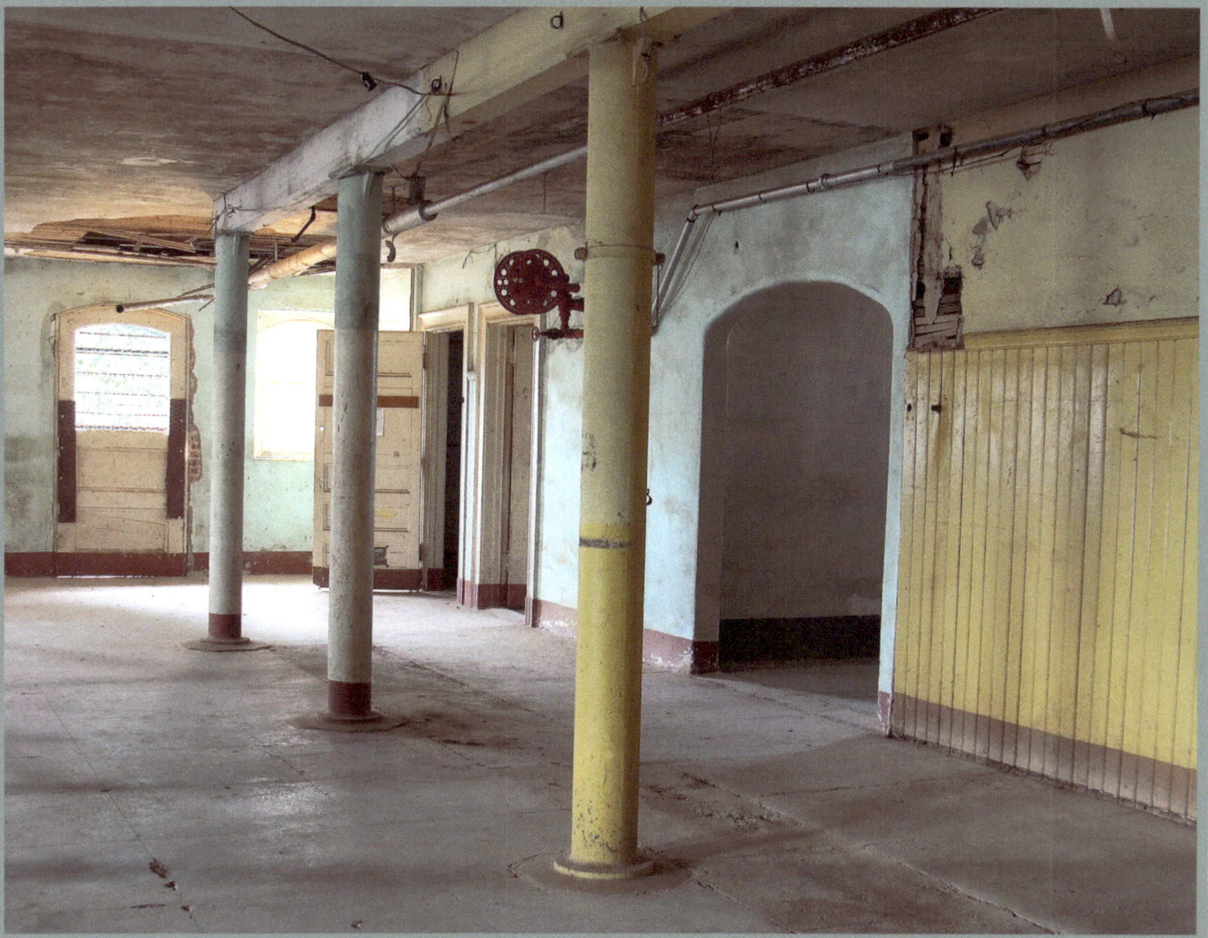

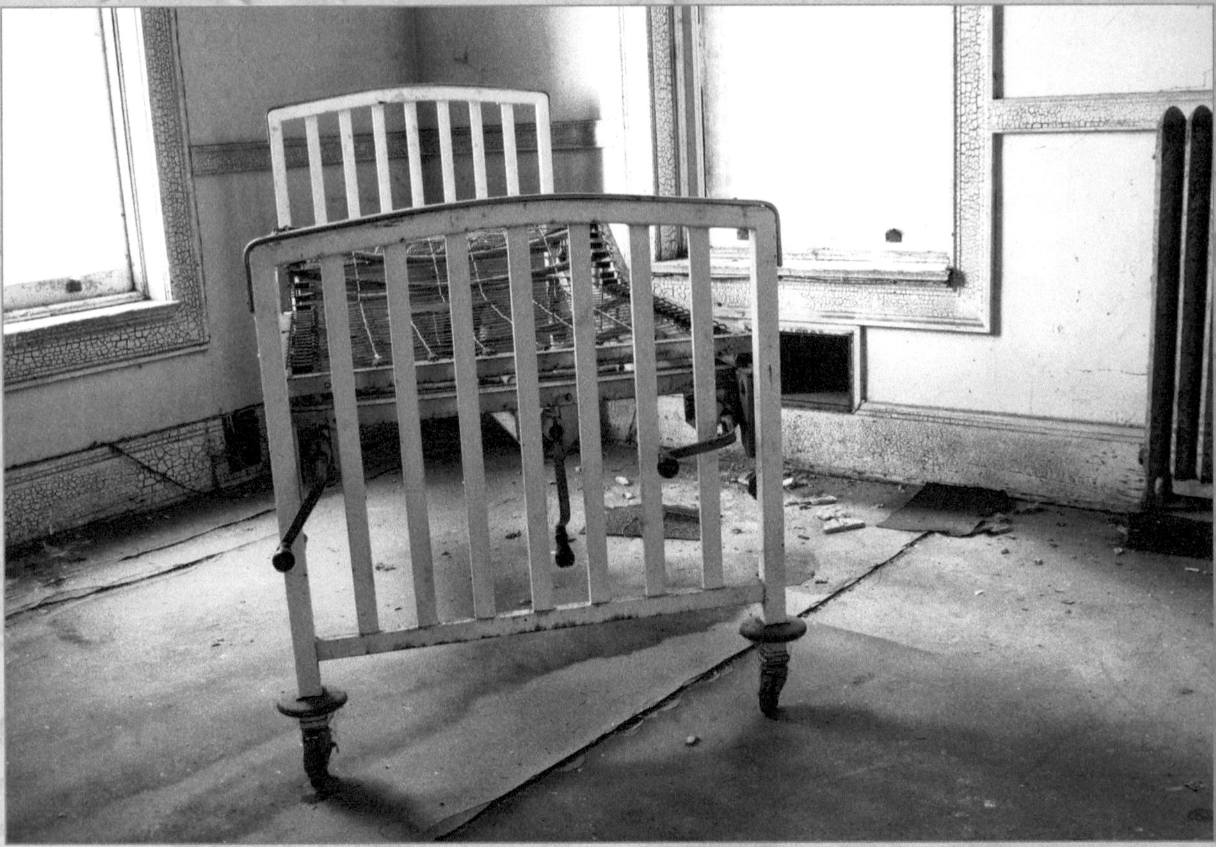

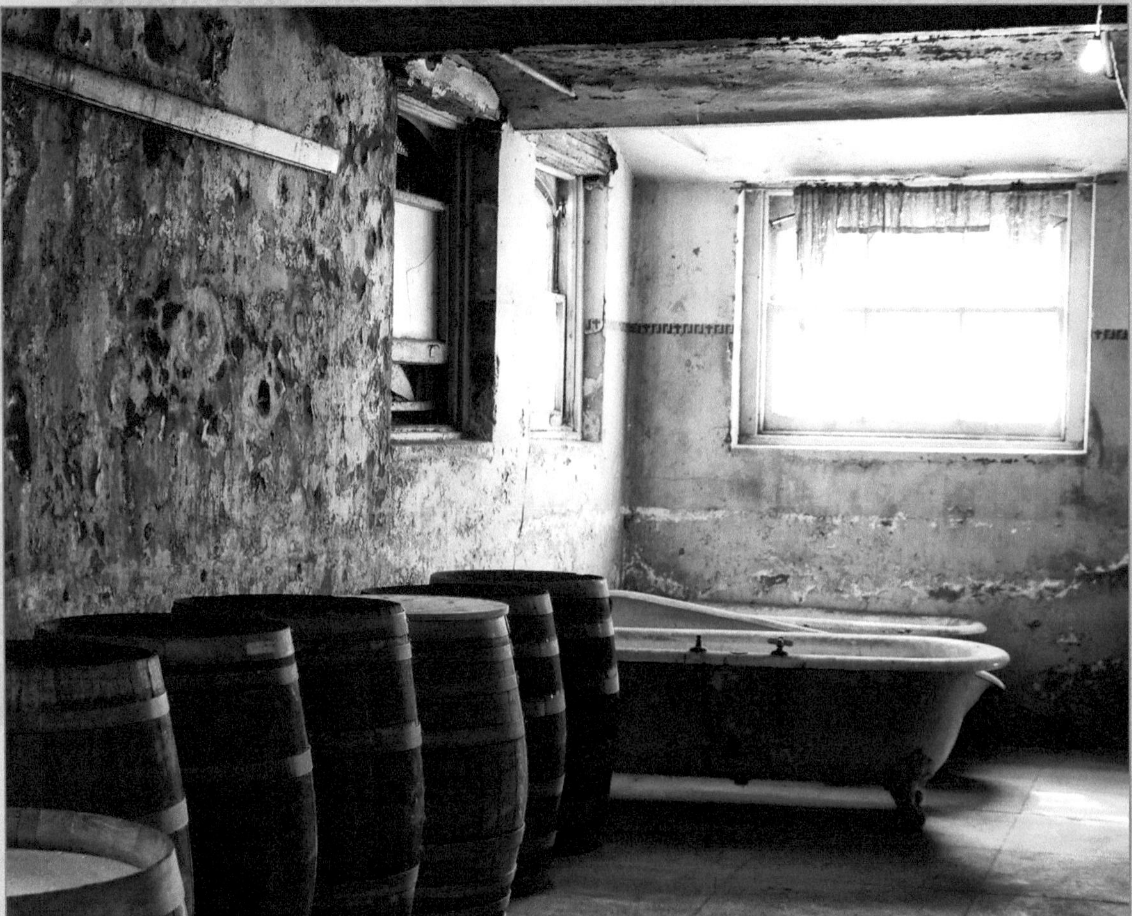

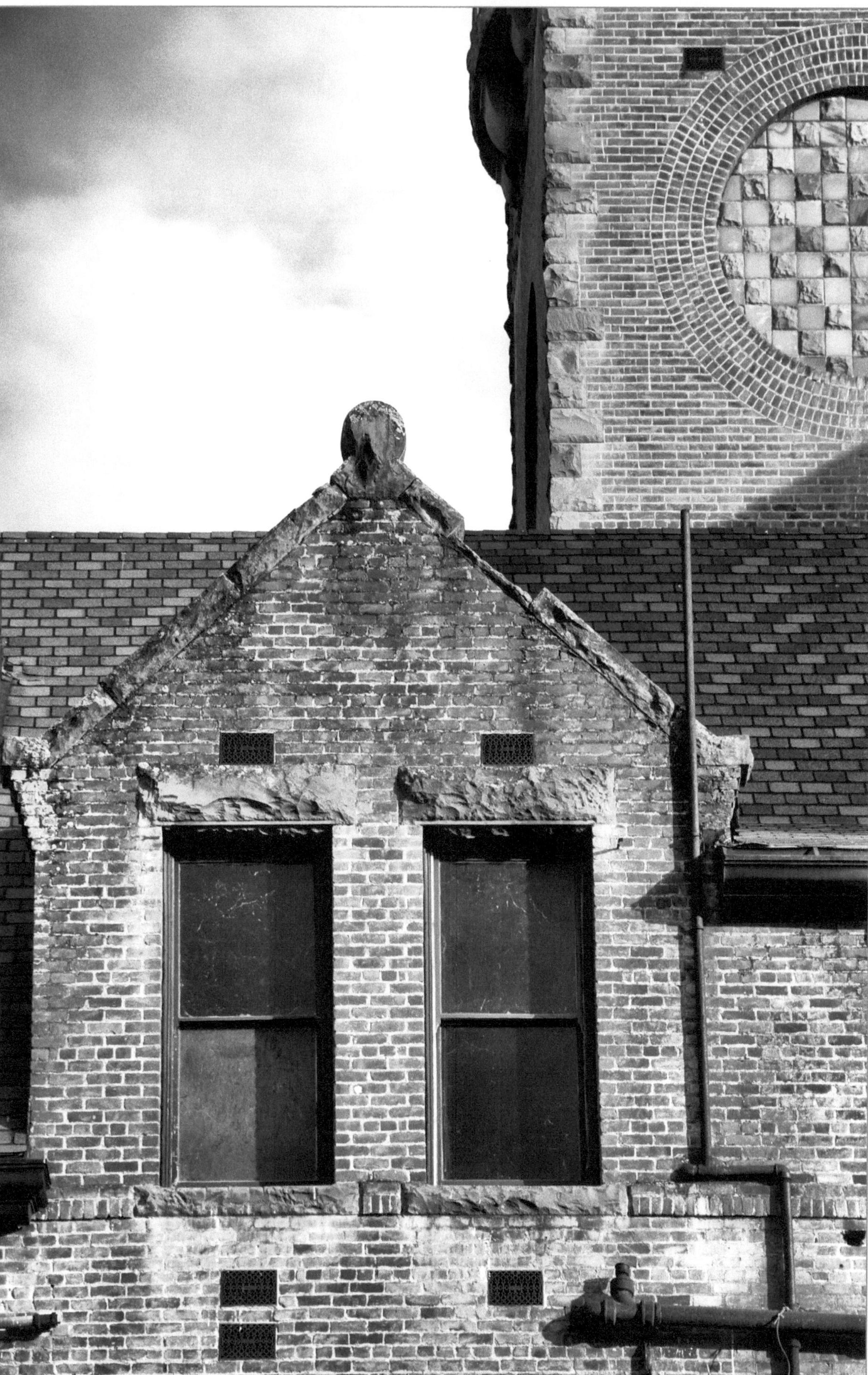

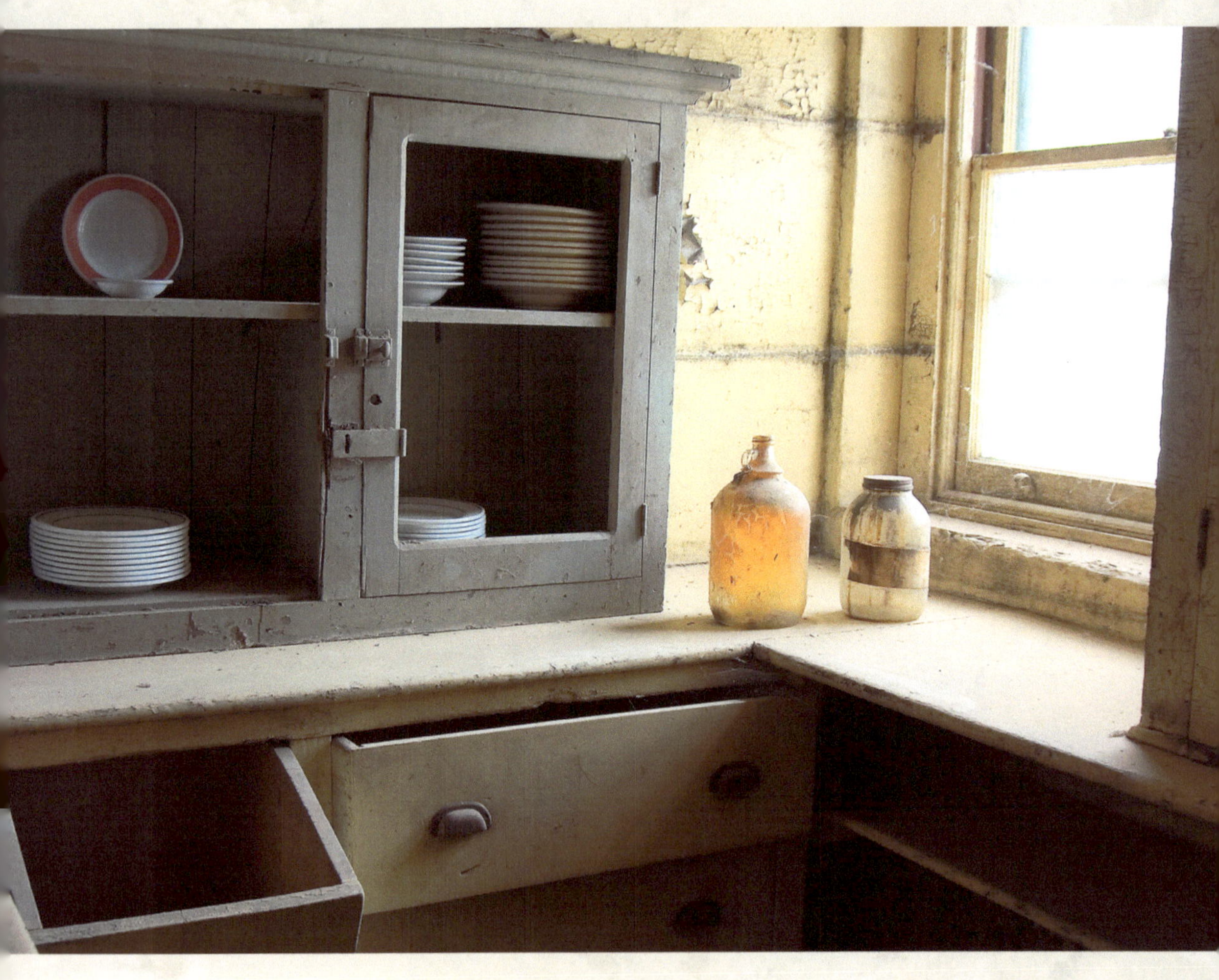

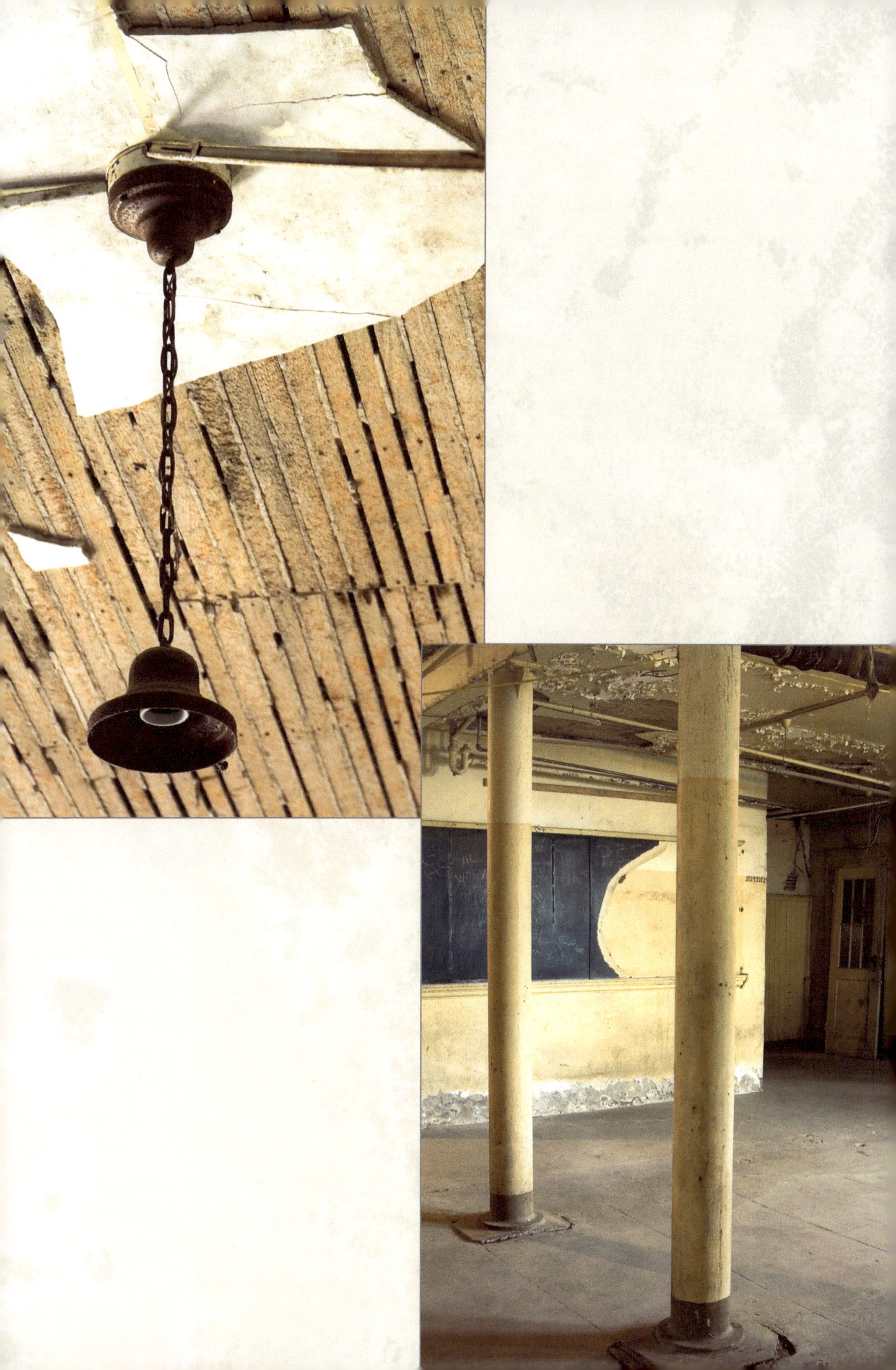

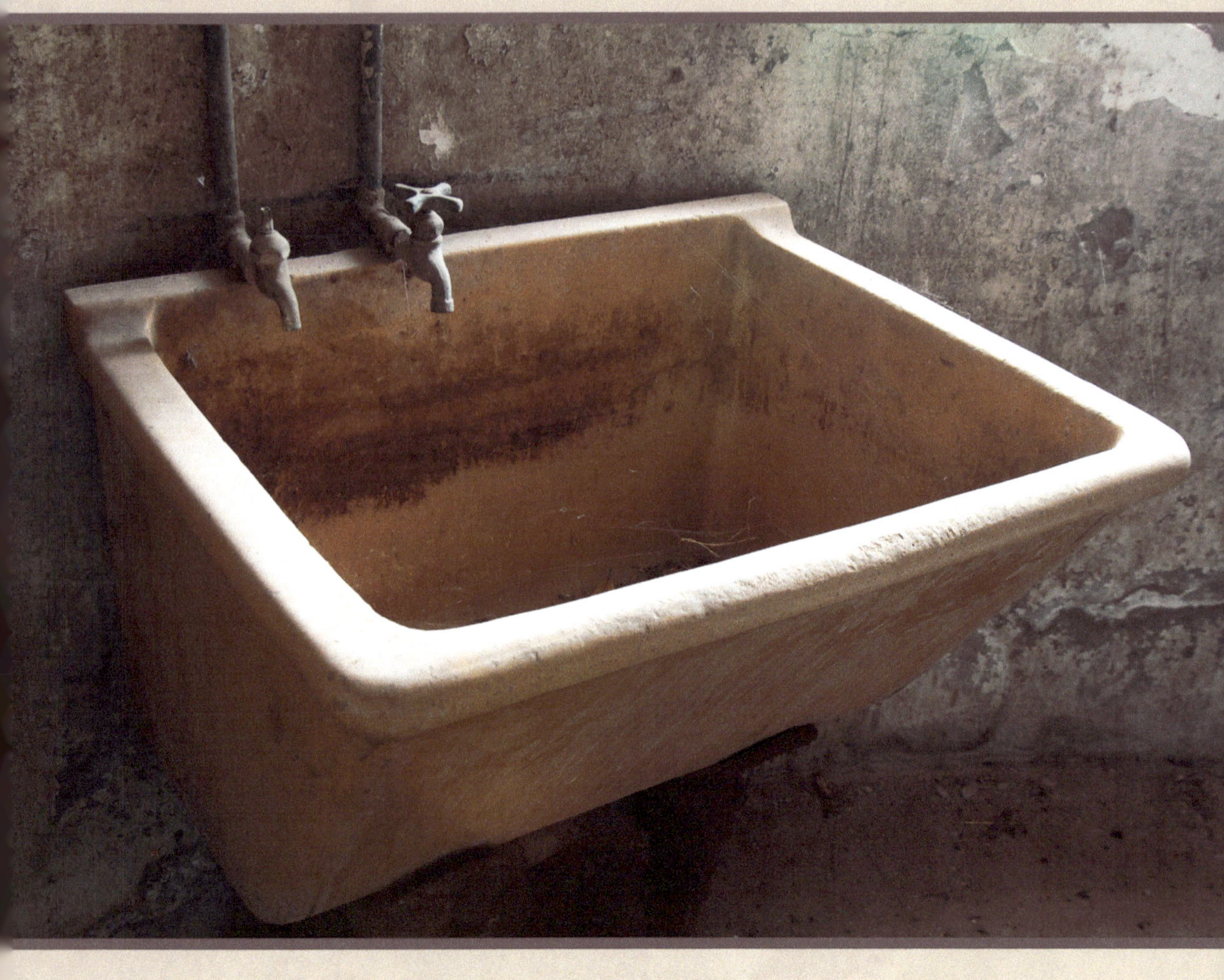

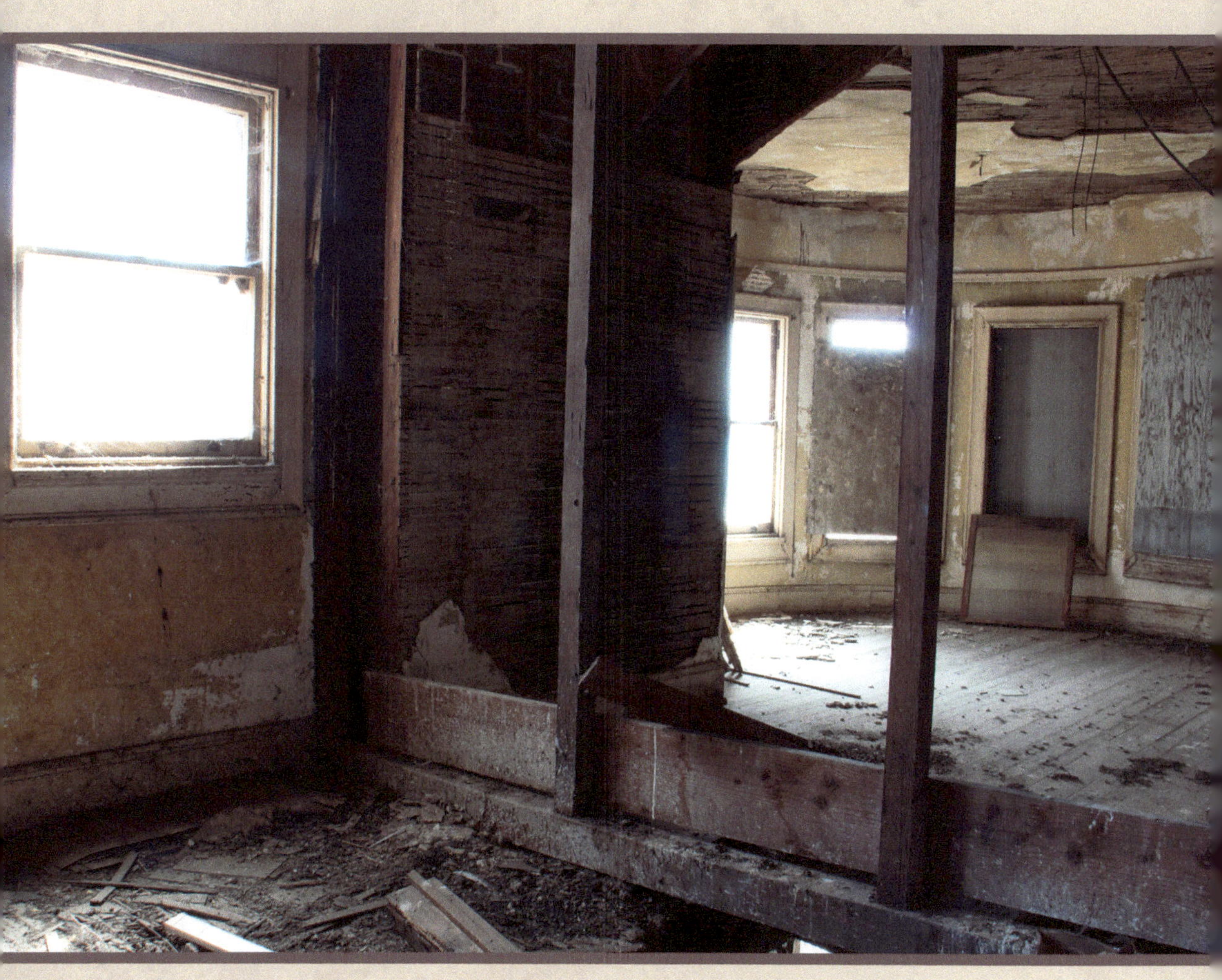

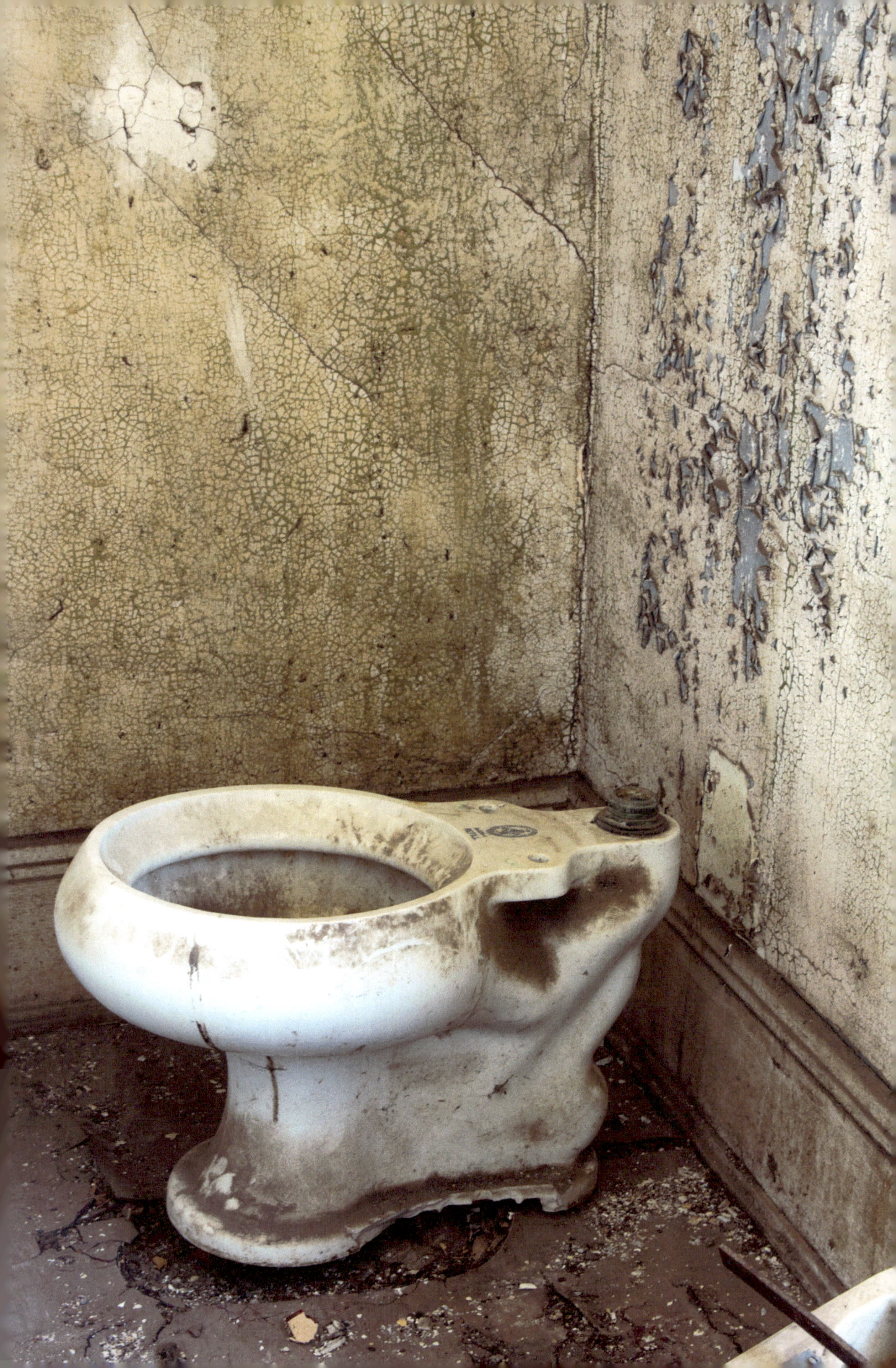

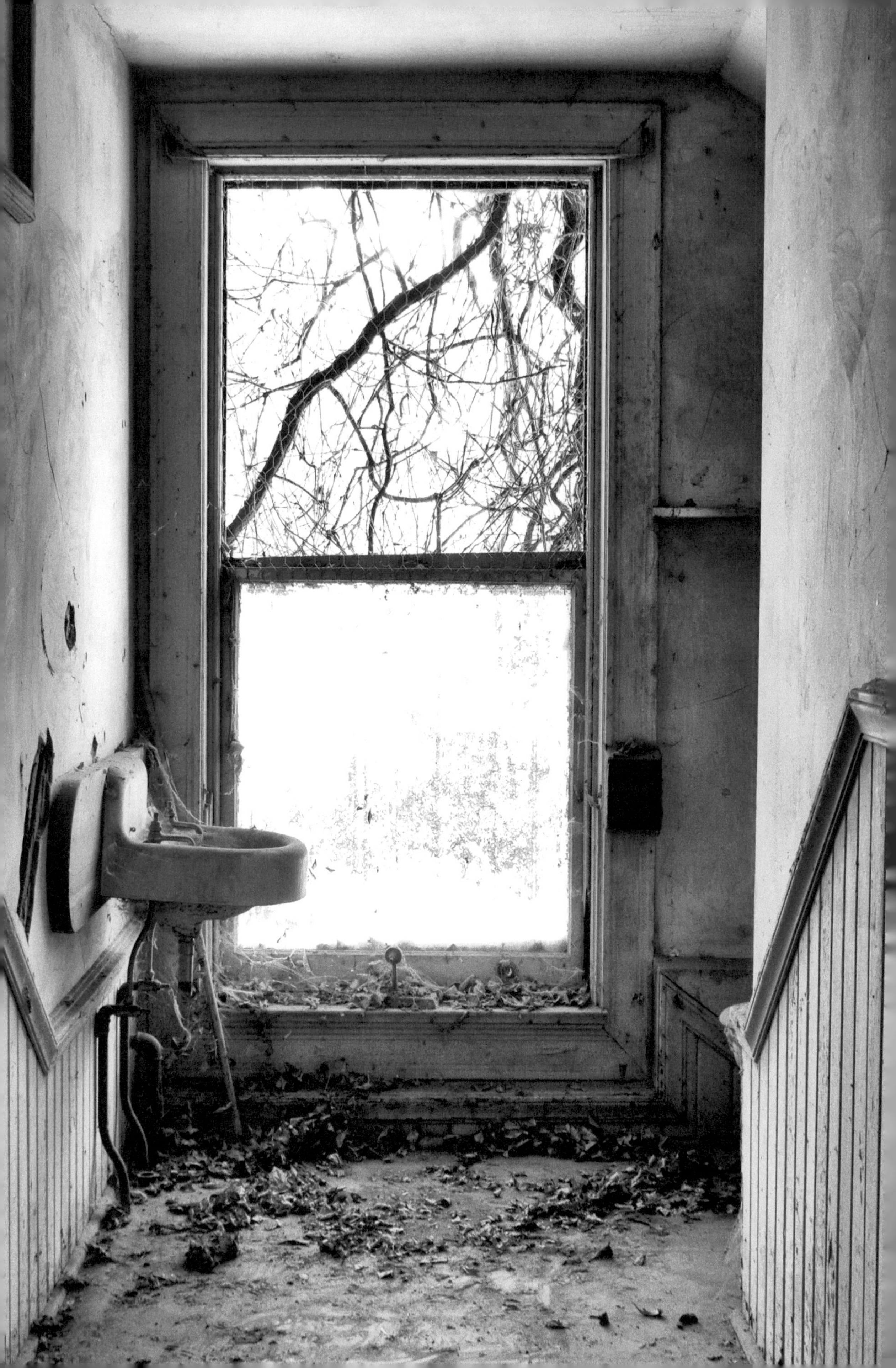

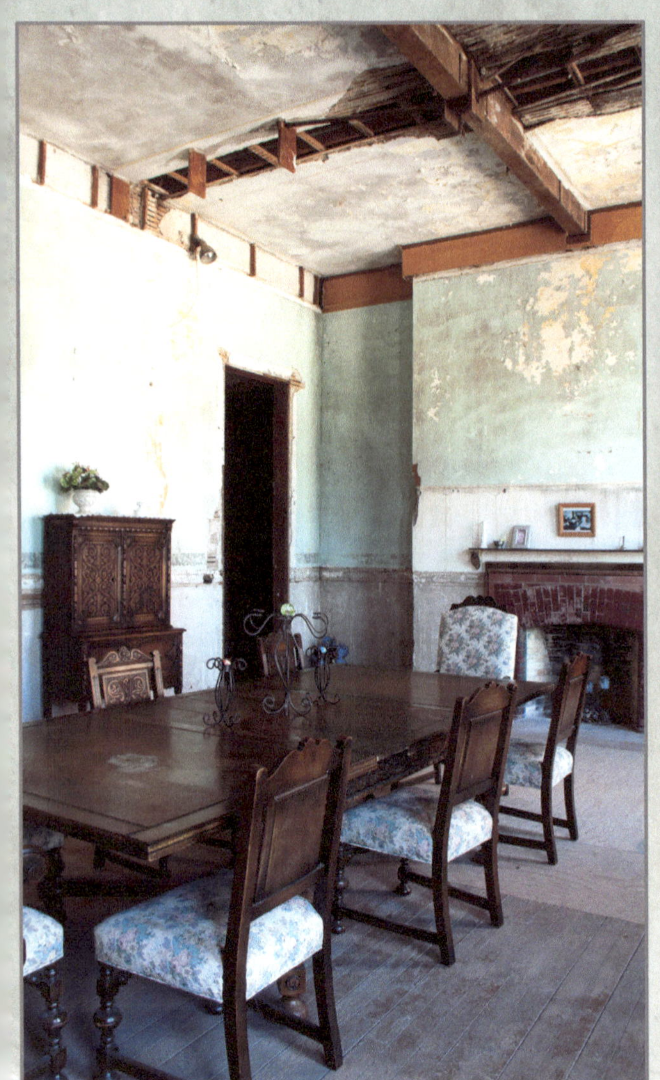
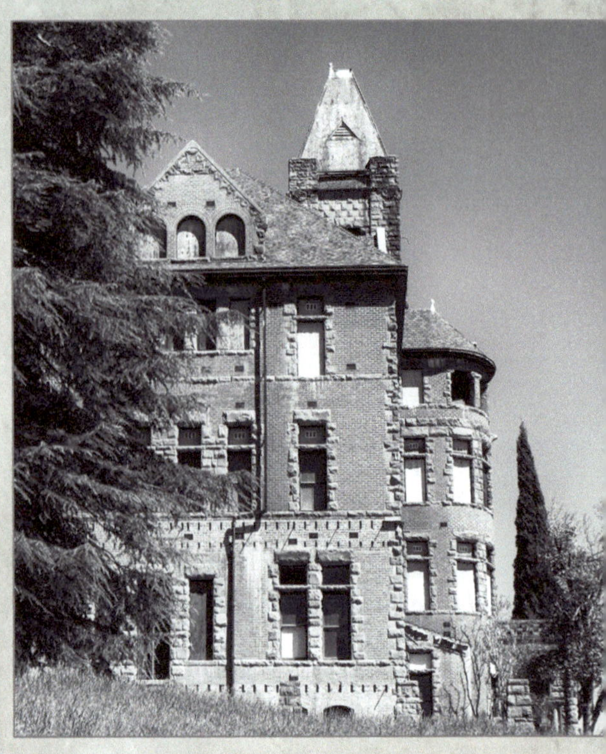
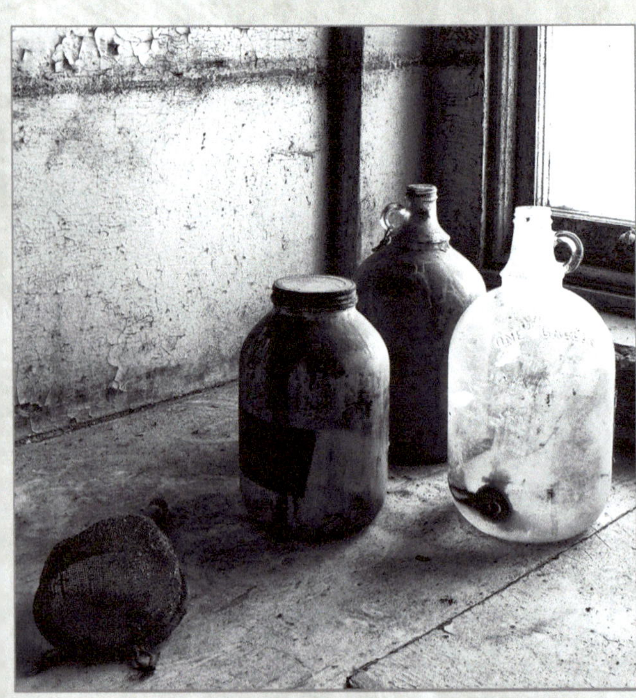
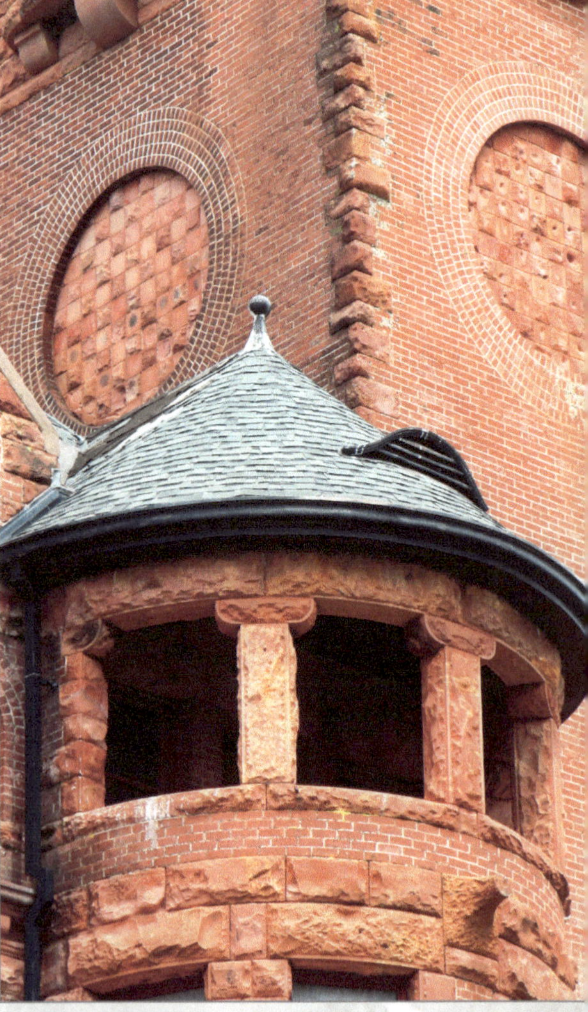

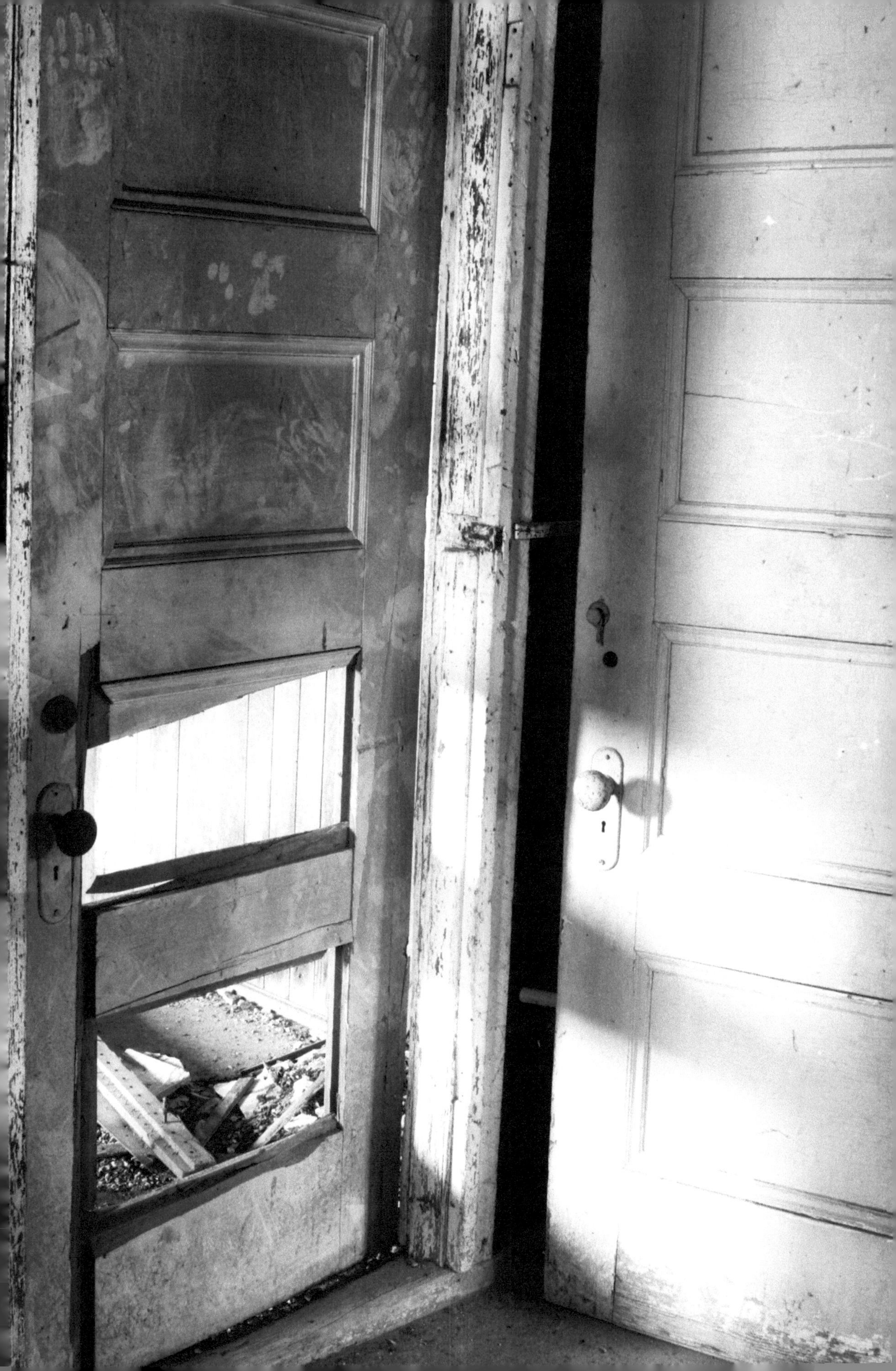

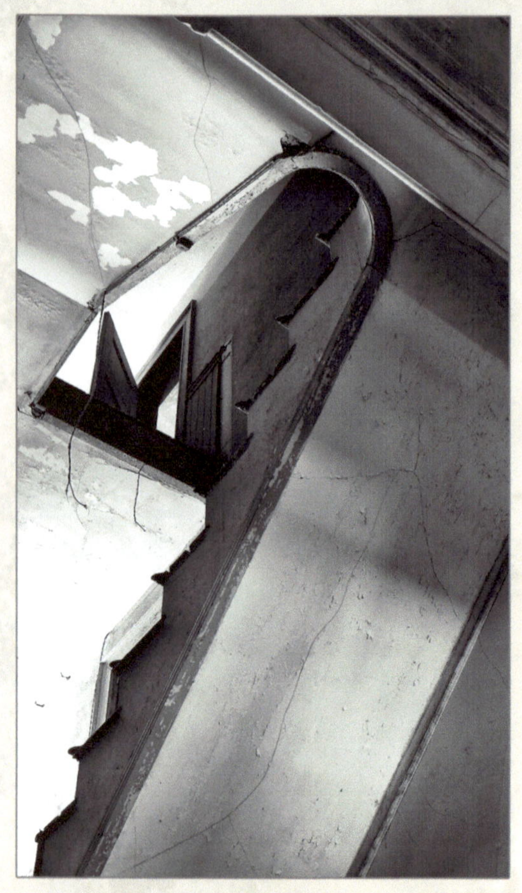

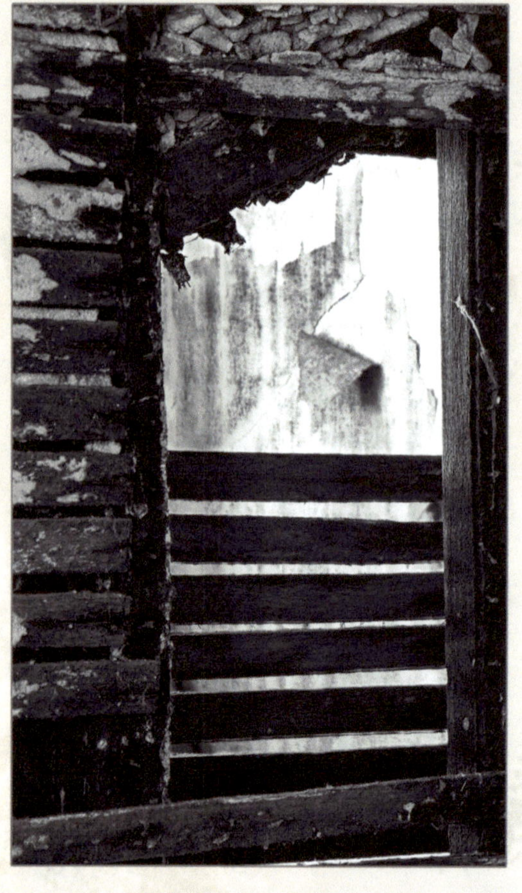

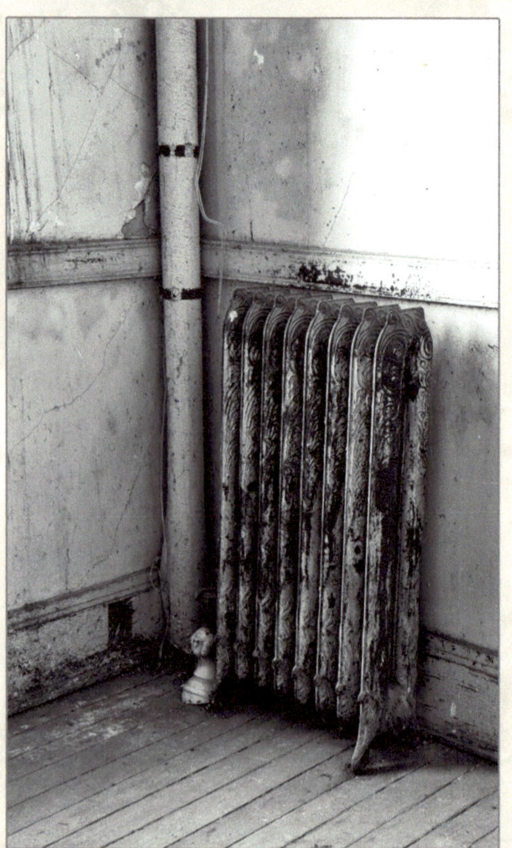

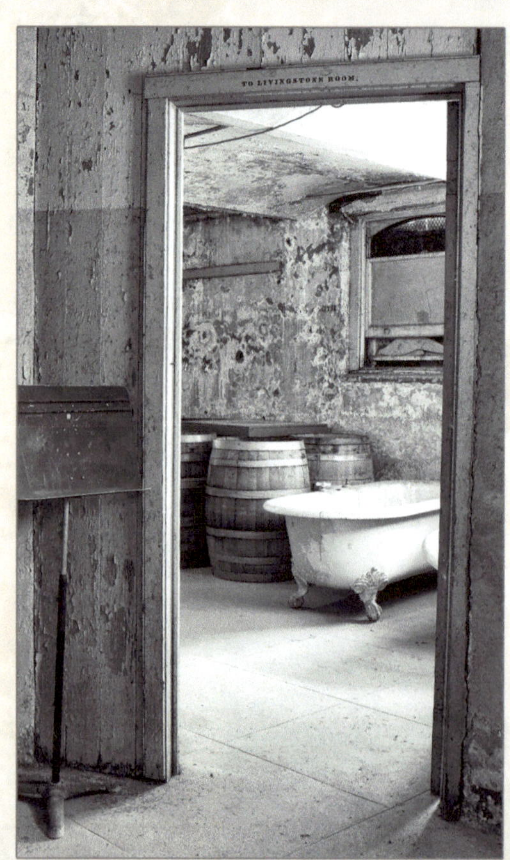
TO LIVINGSTONE ROOM.

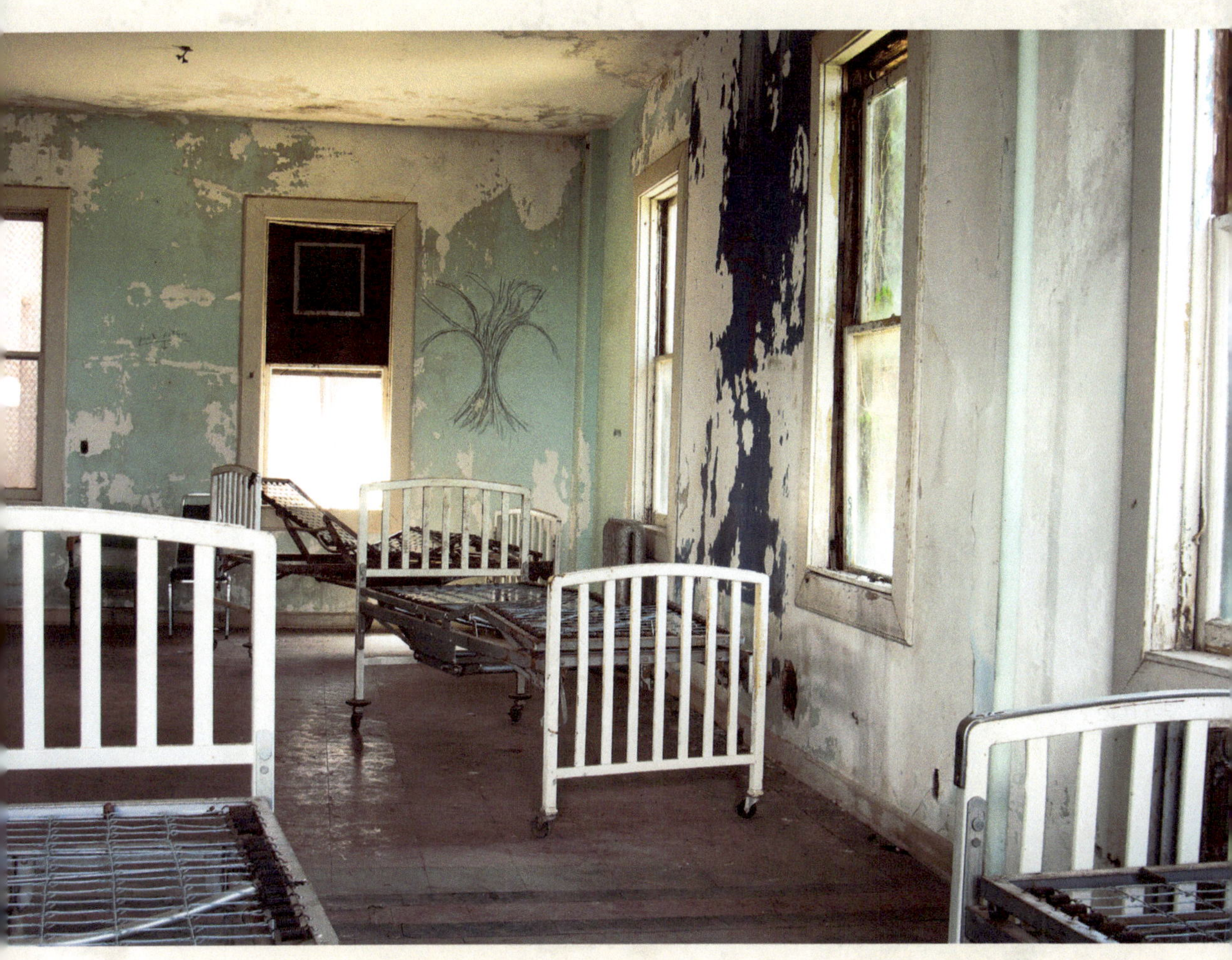

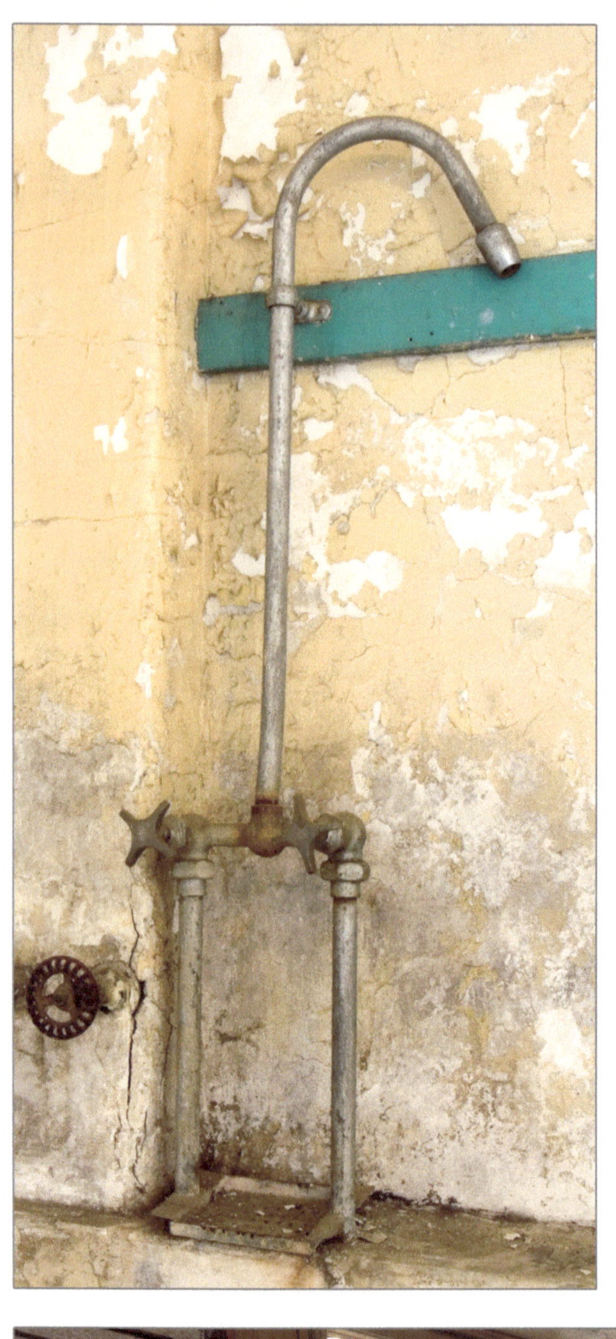

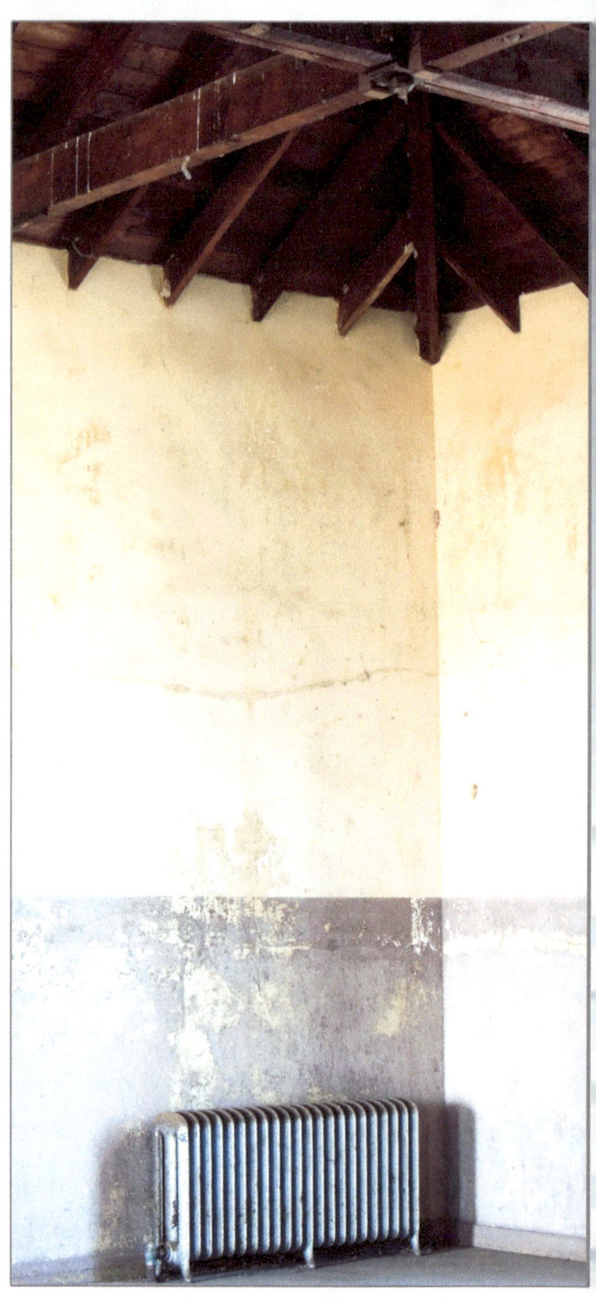

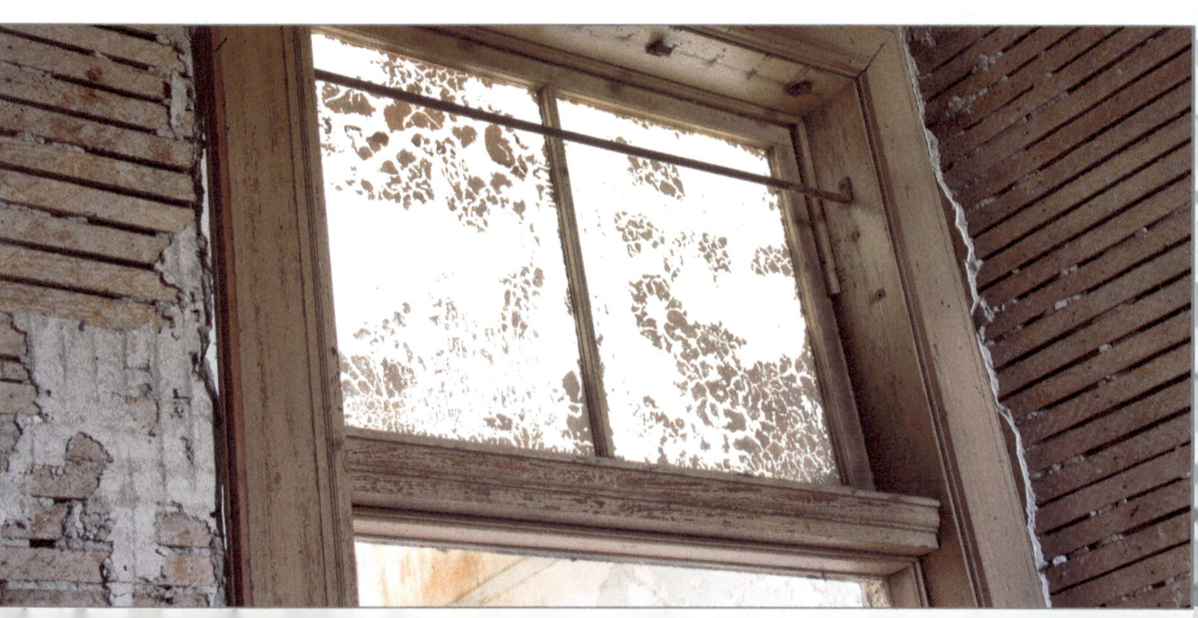

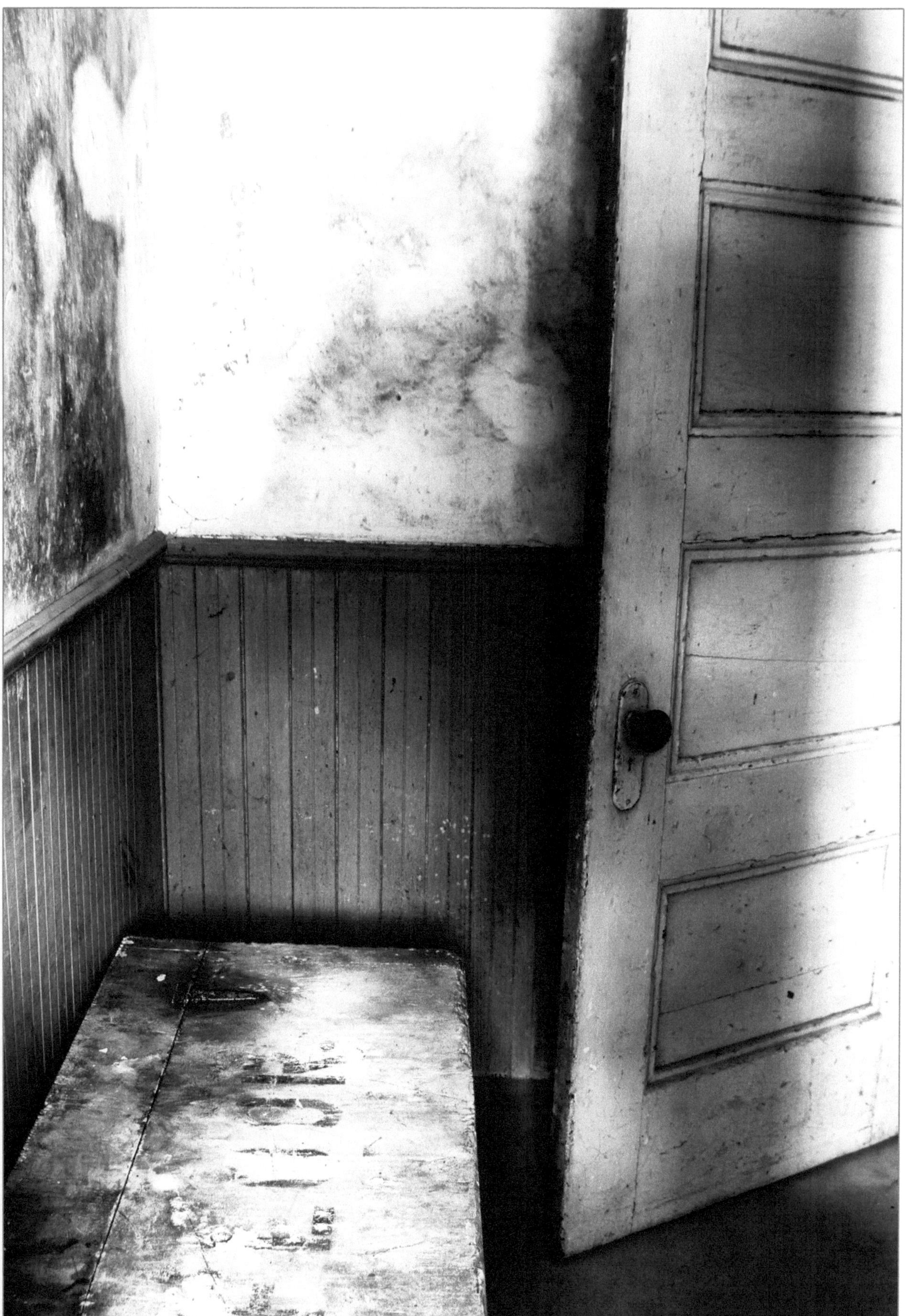

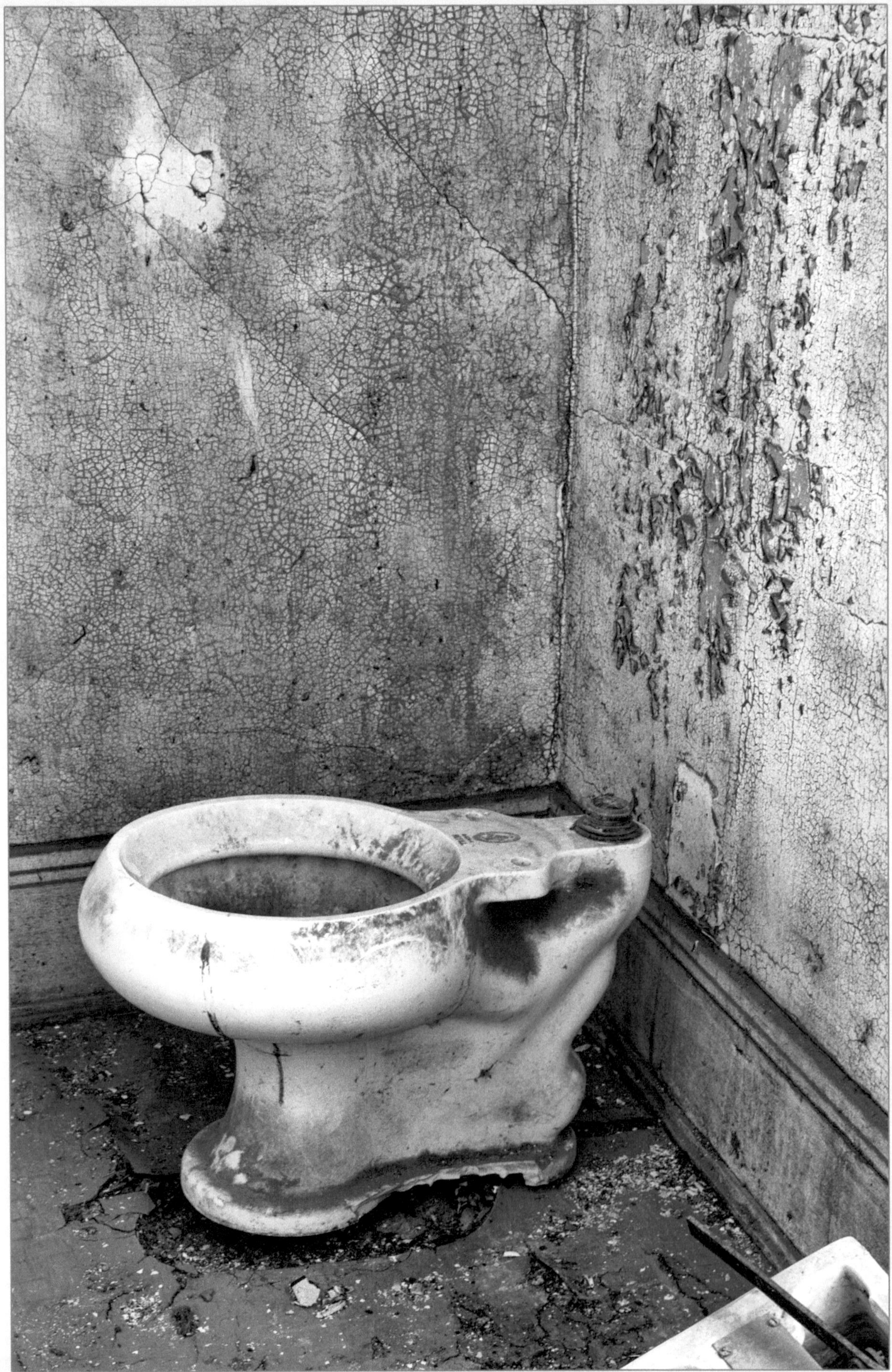

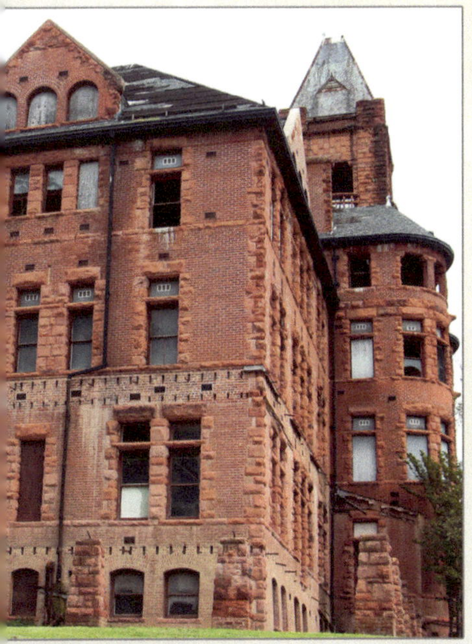

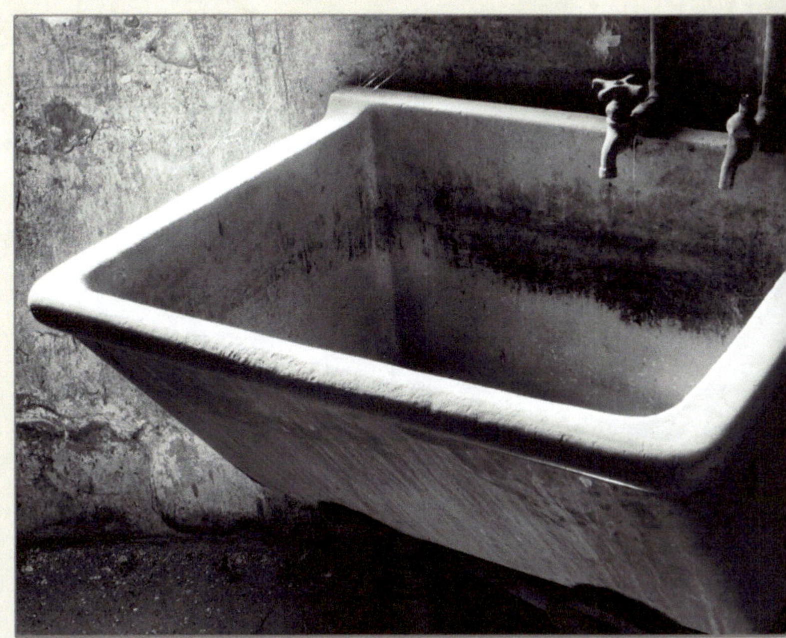

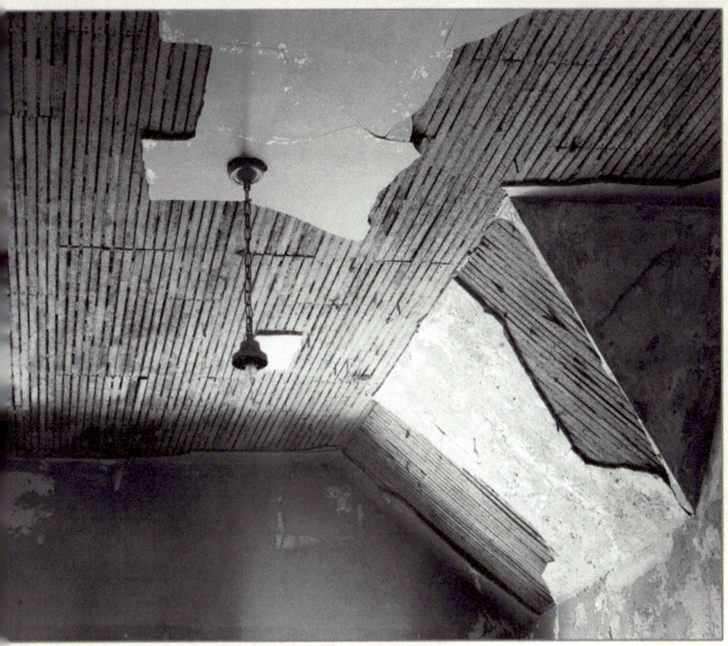

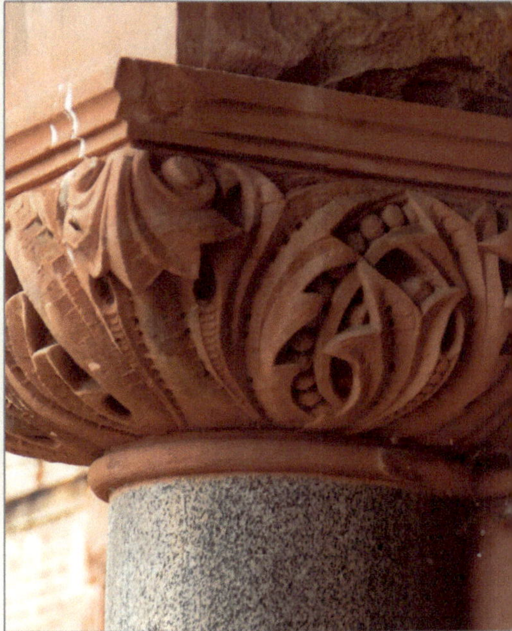

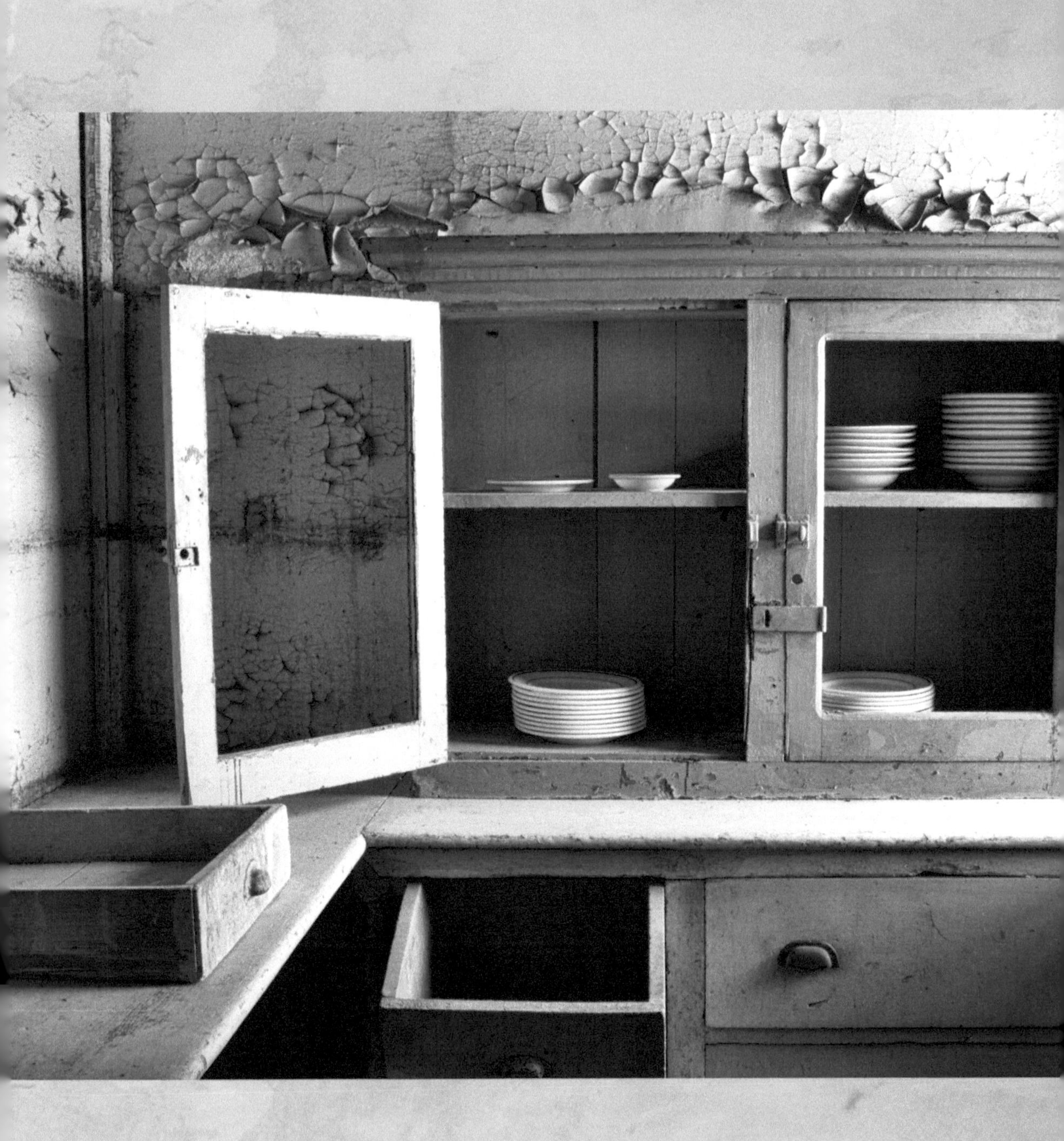

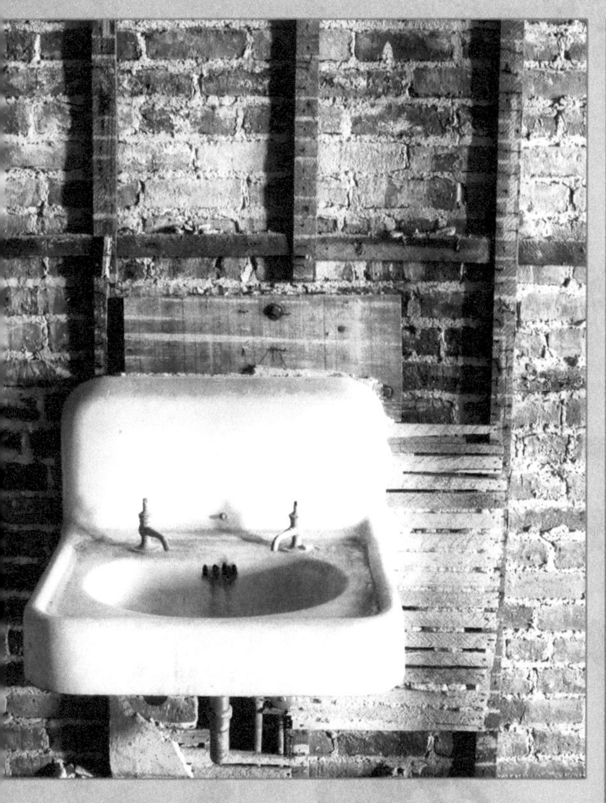

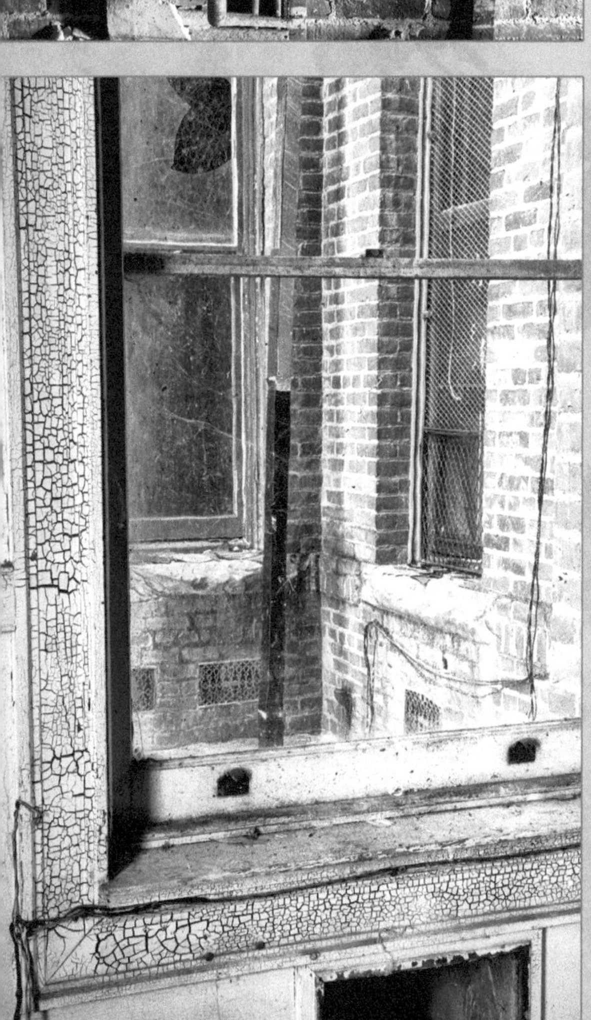

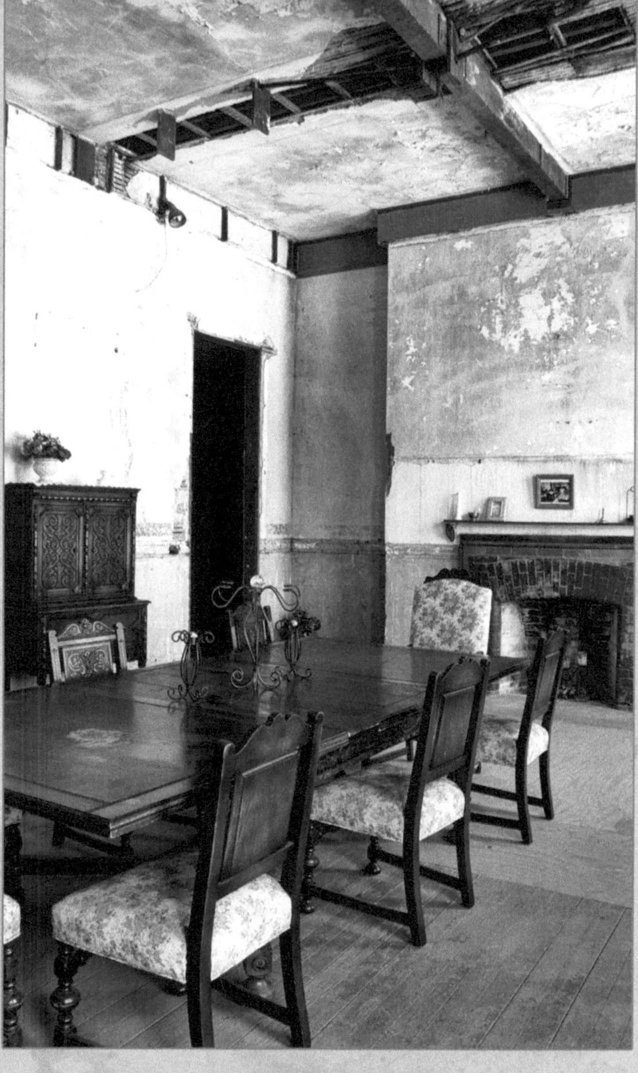

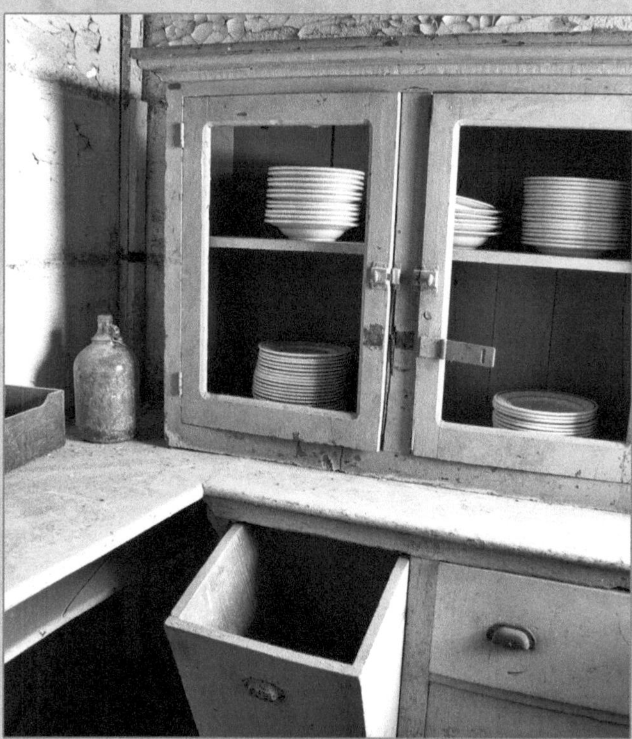

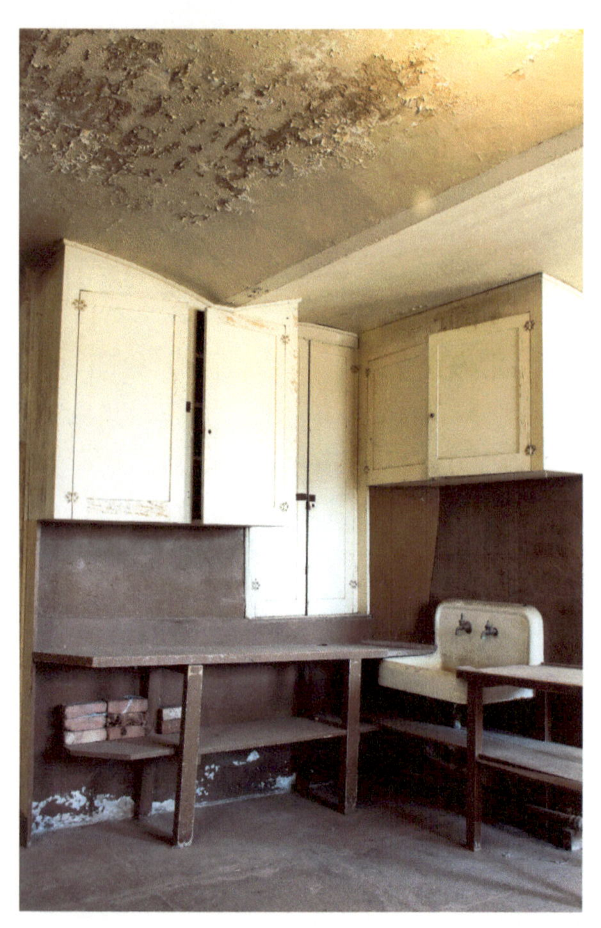
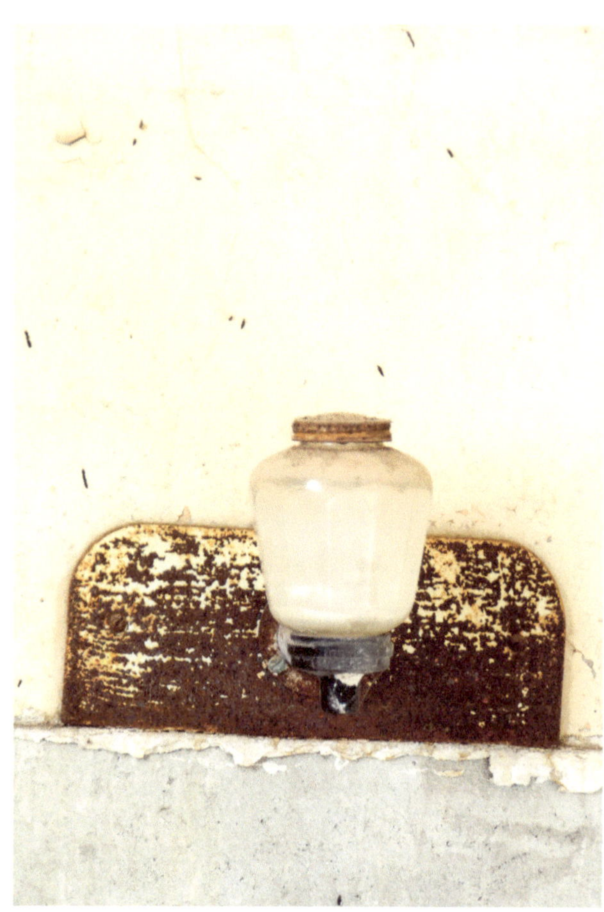

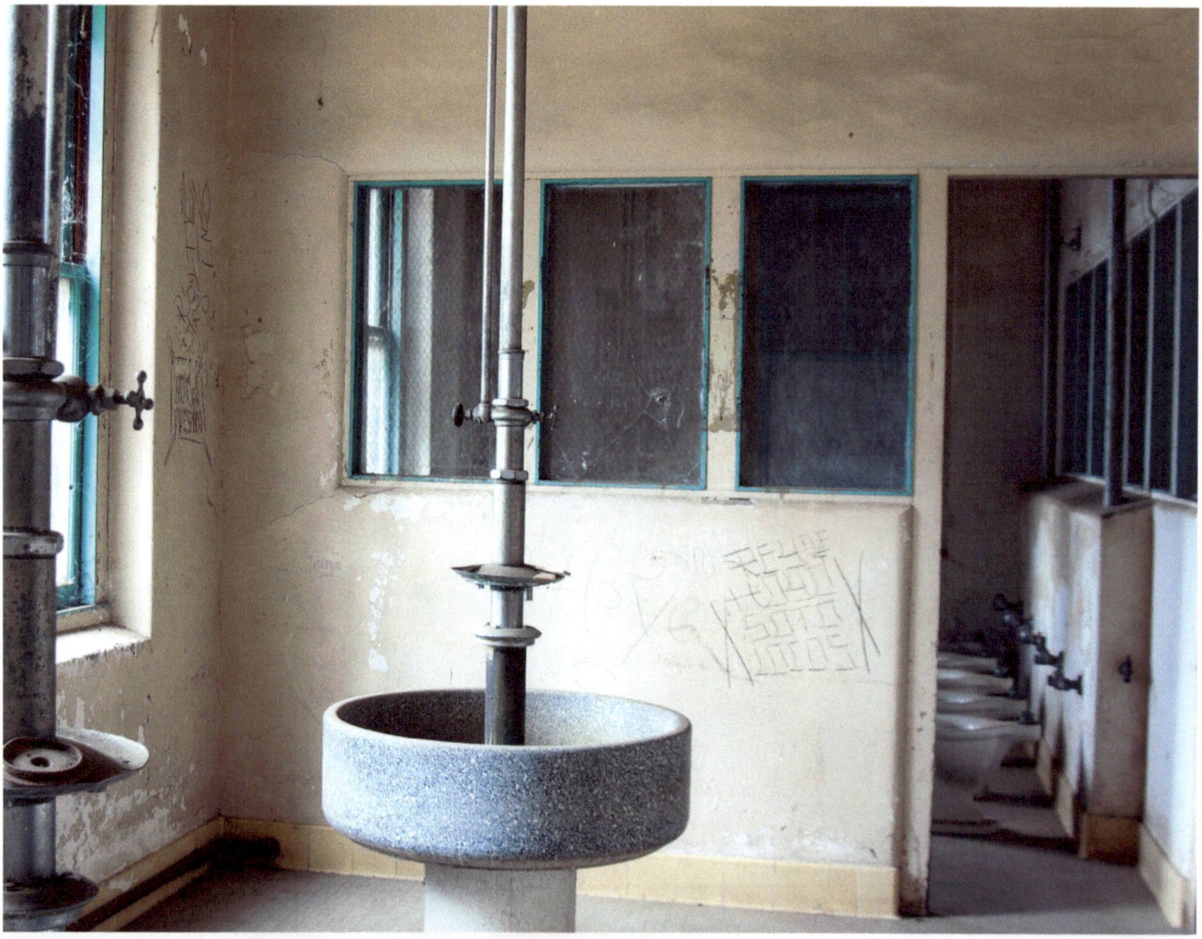

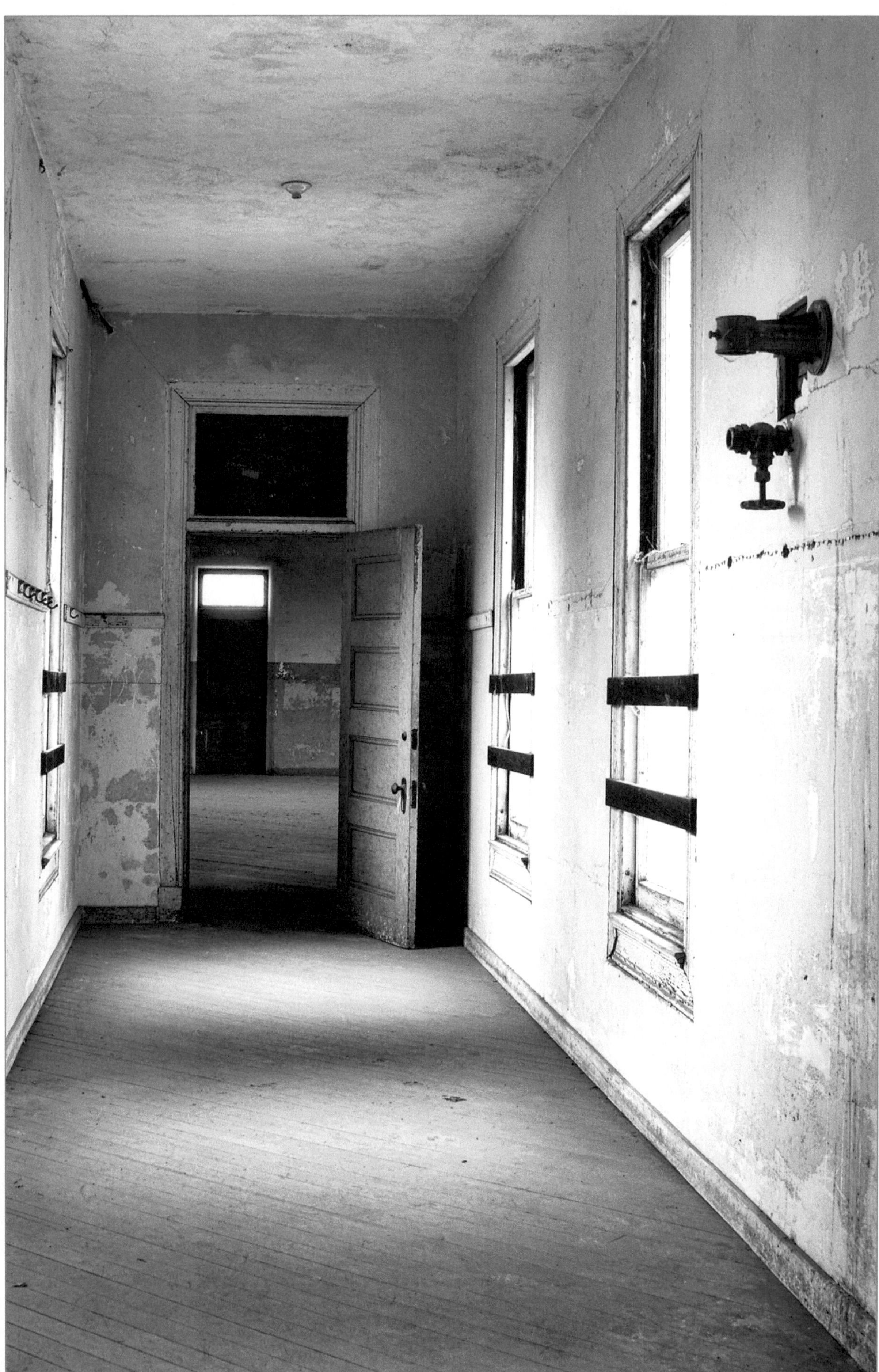

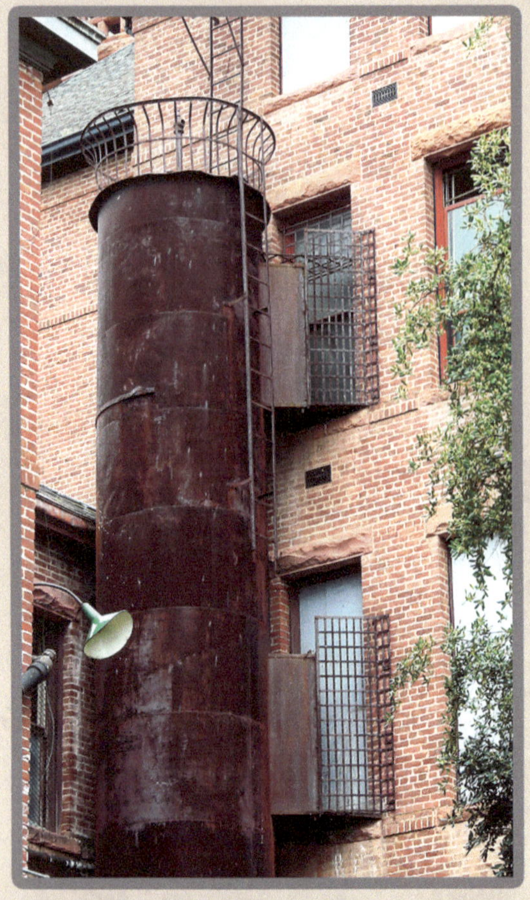

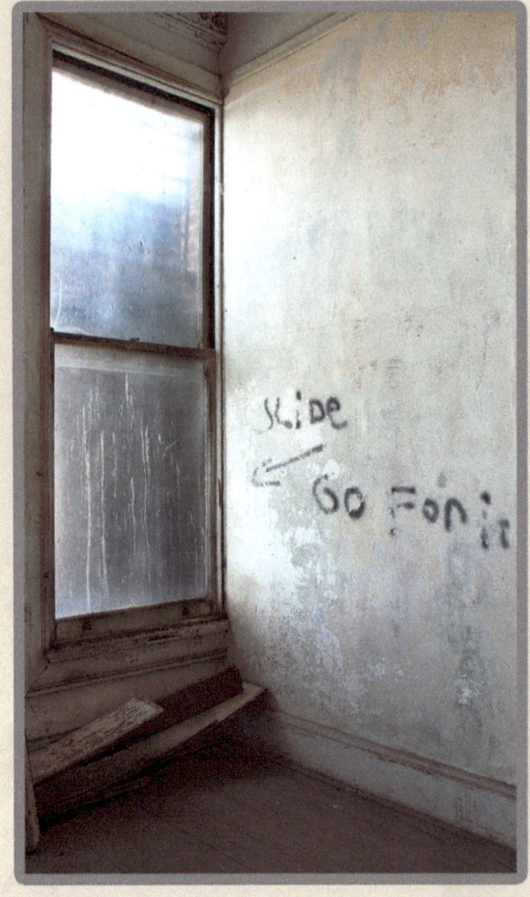
Slide
Go For It

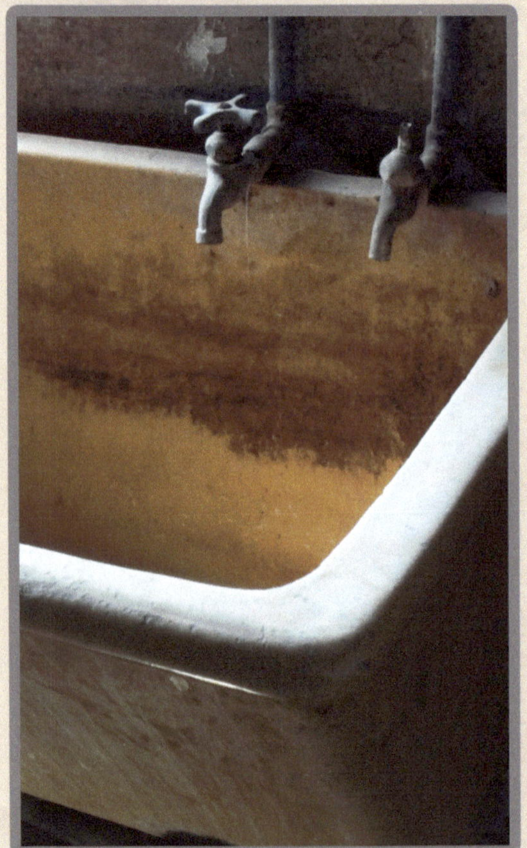

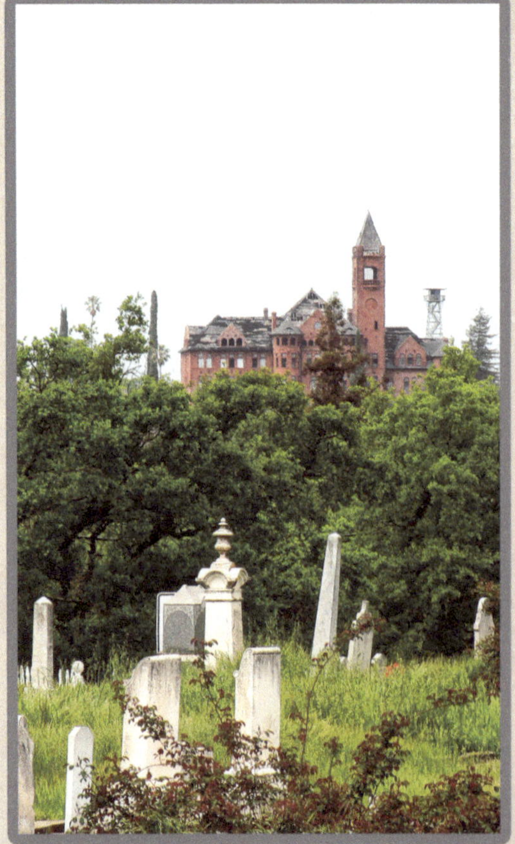

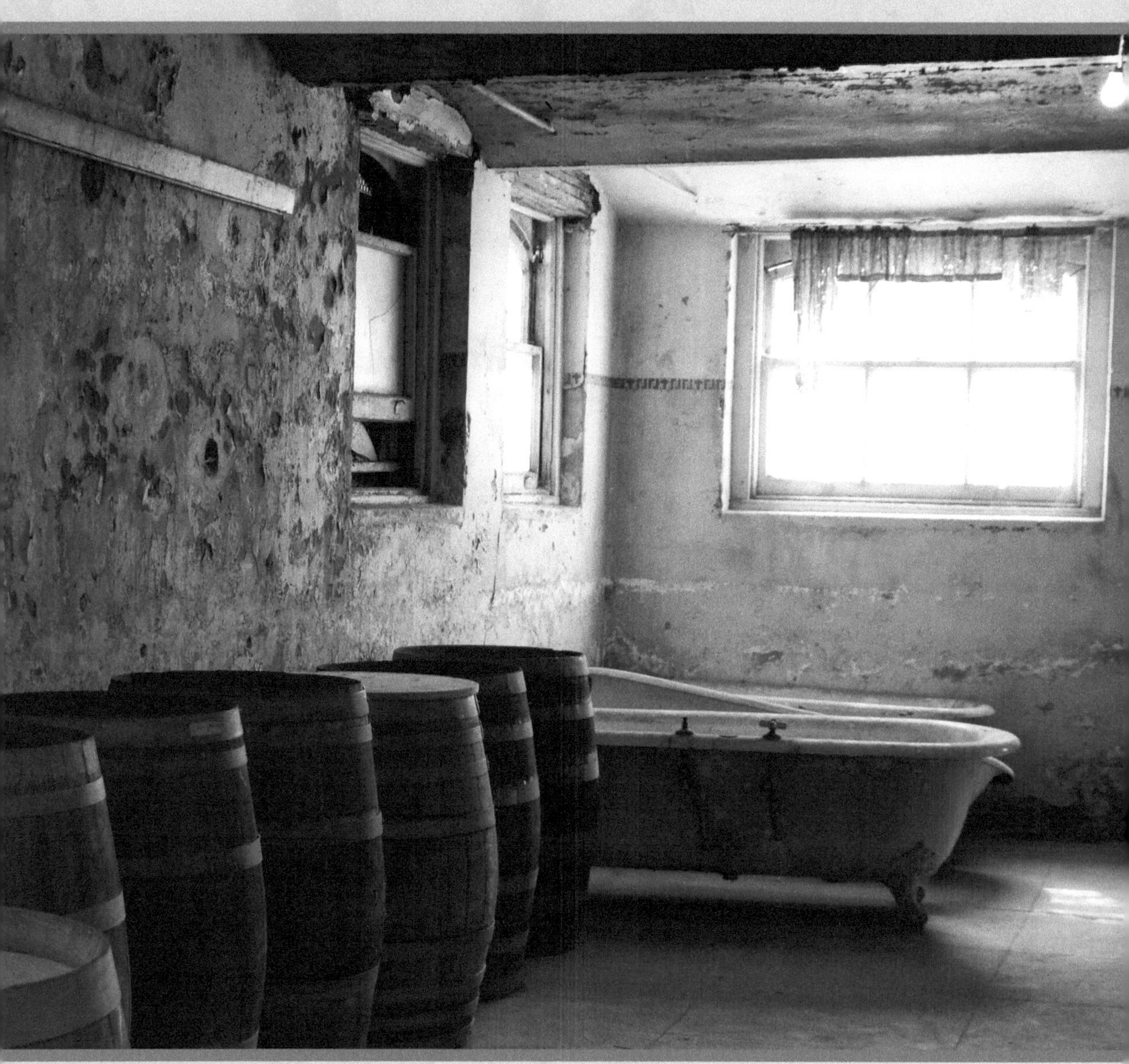

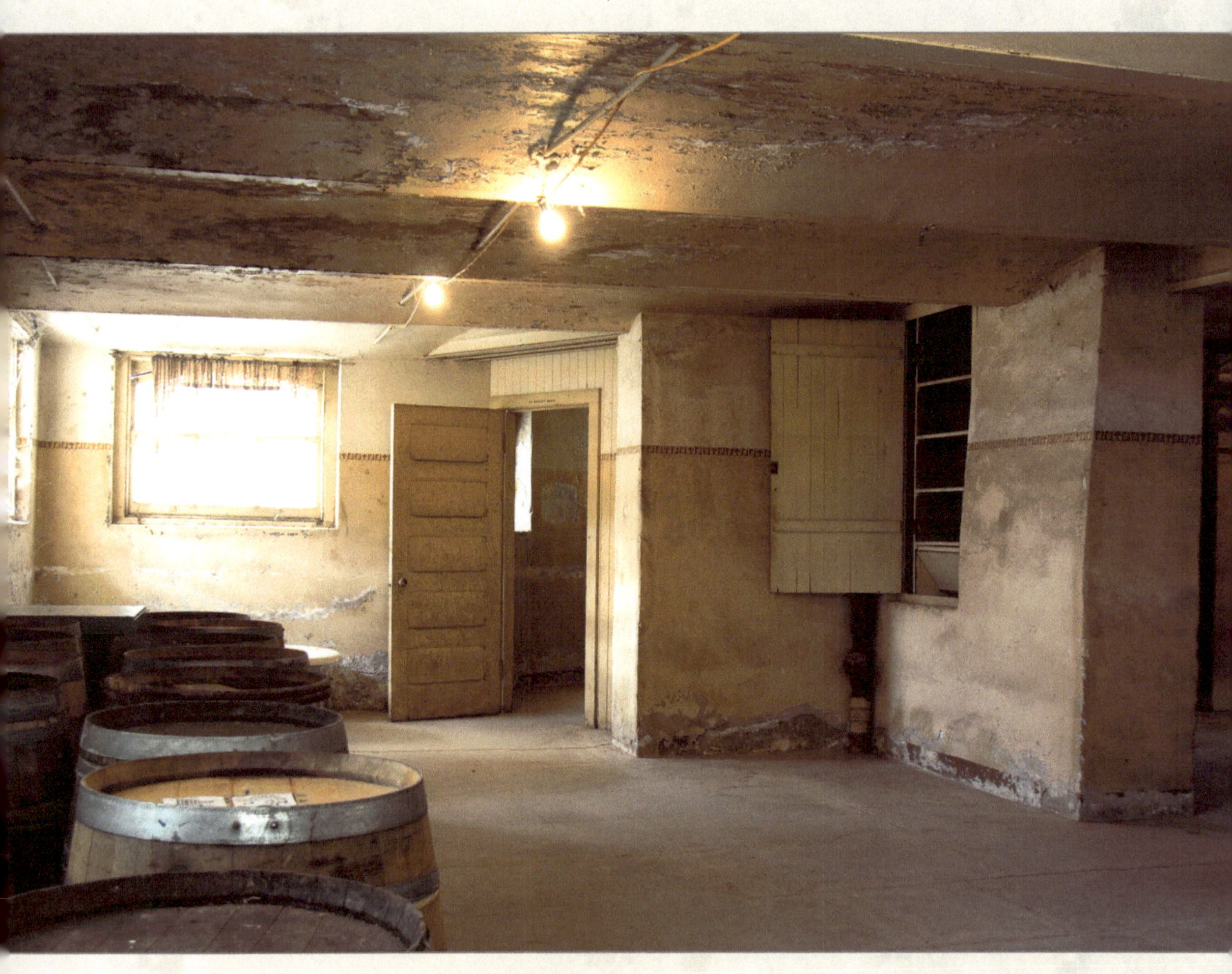

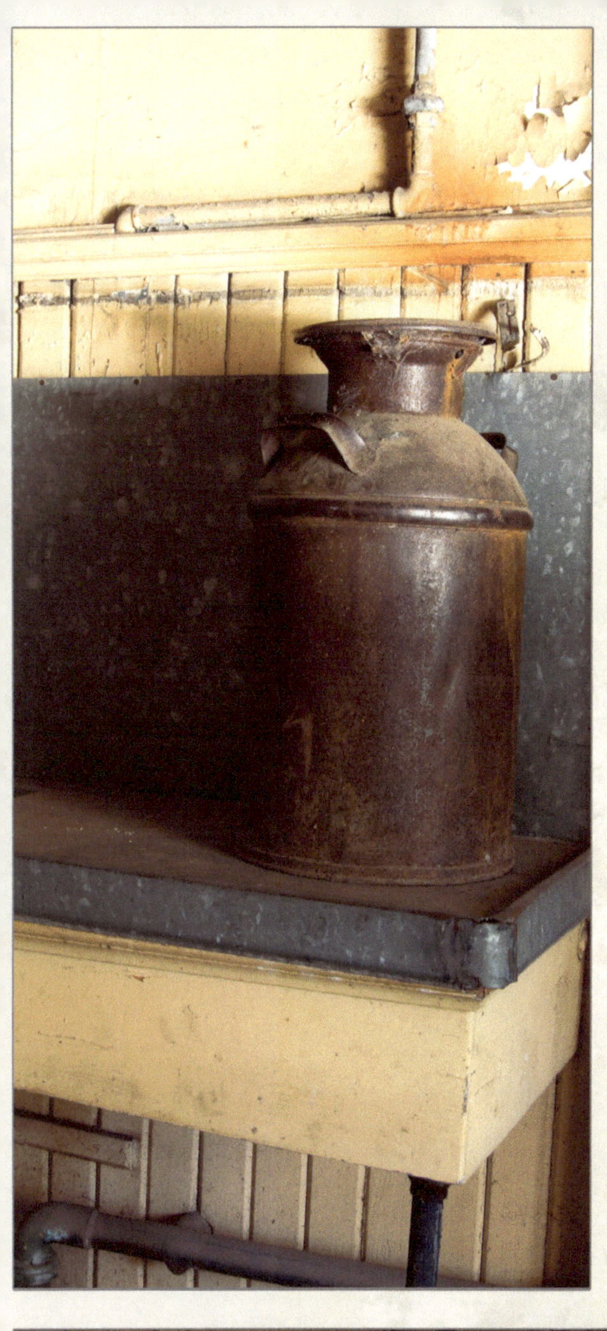

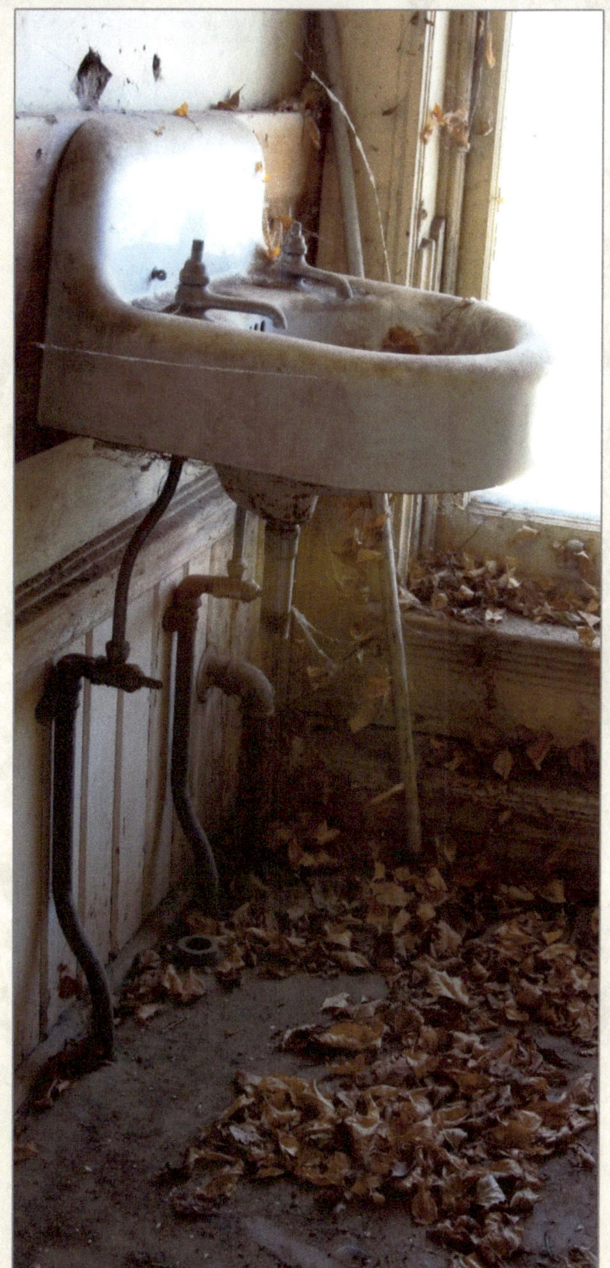

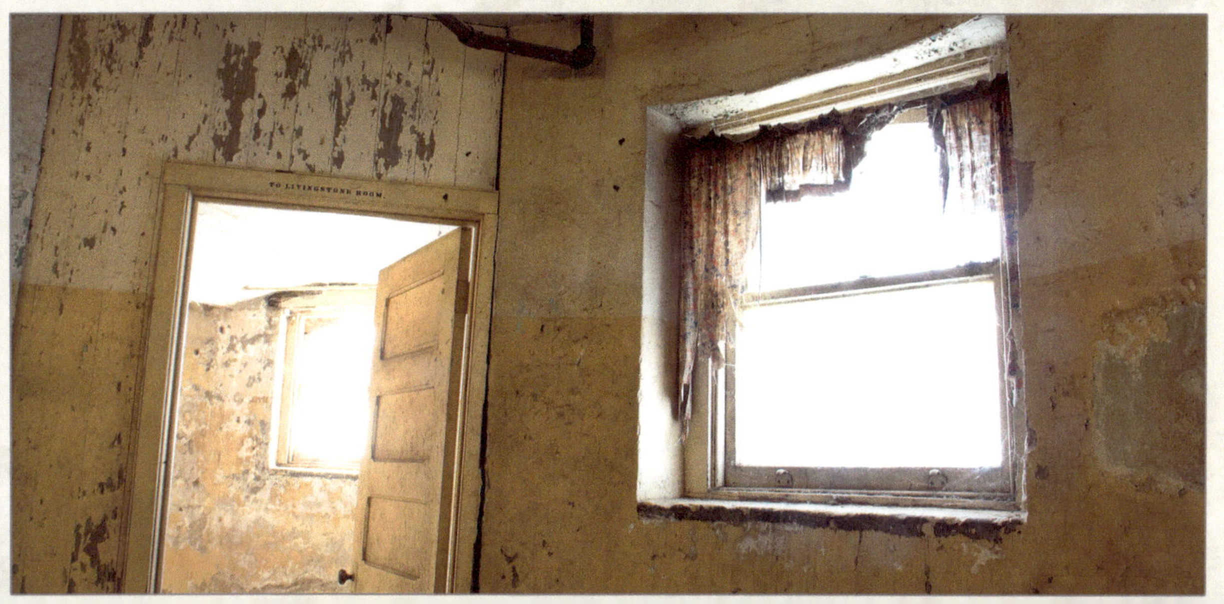
TO LIVINGSTONE ROOM.

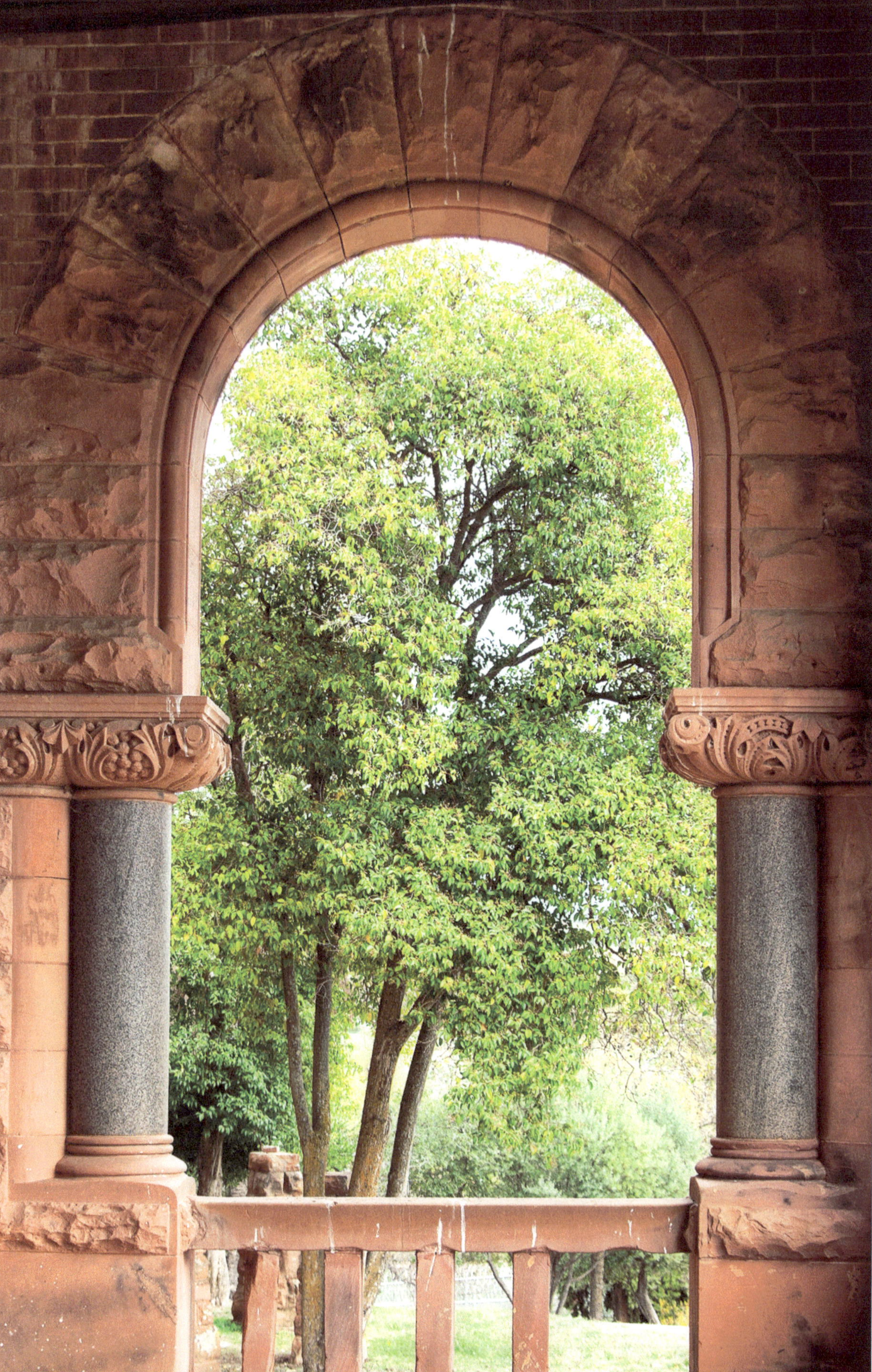

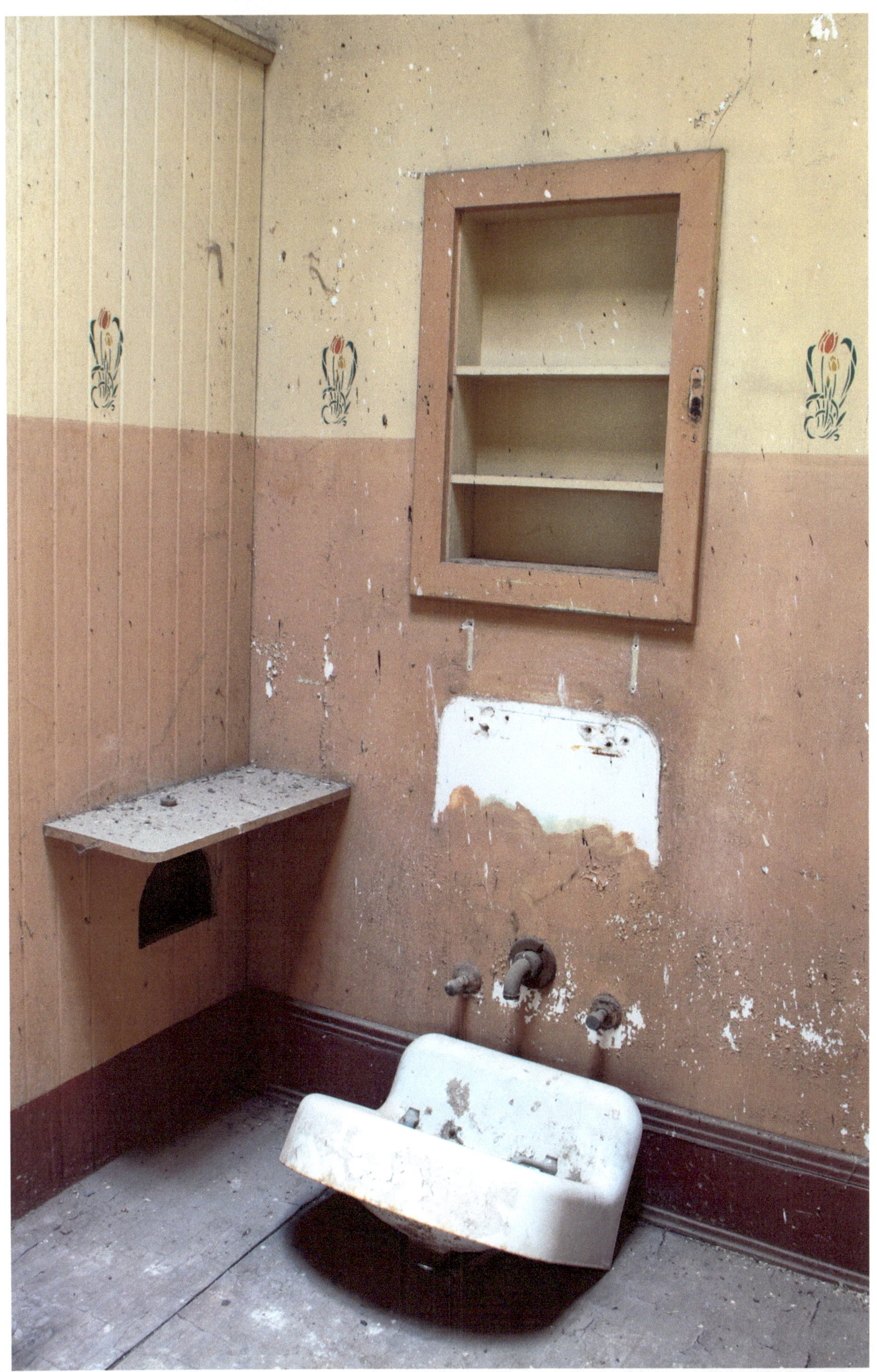

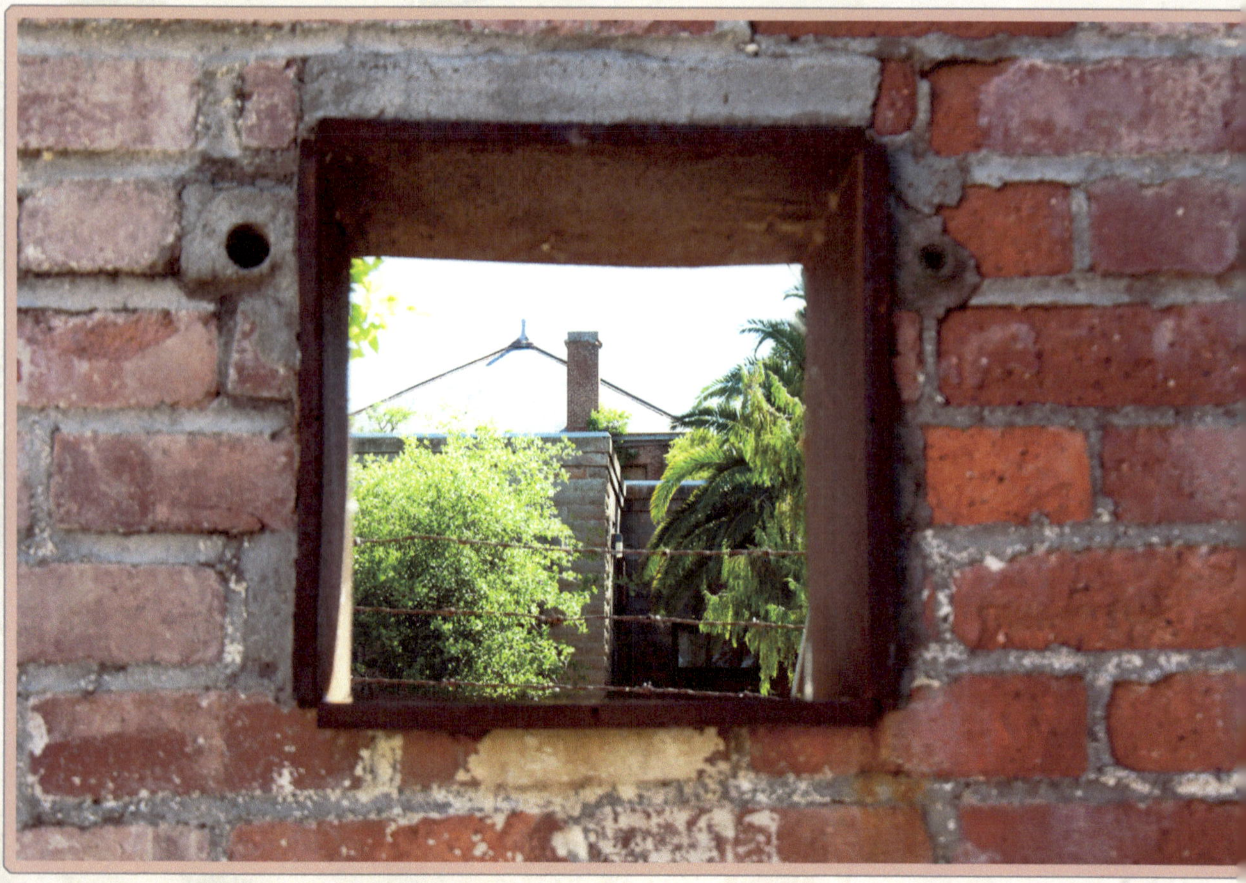

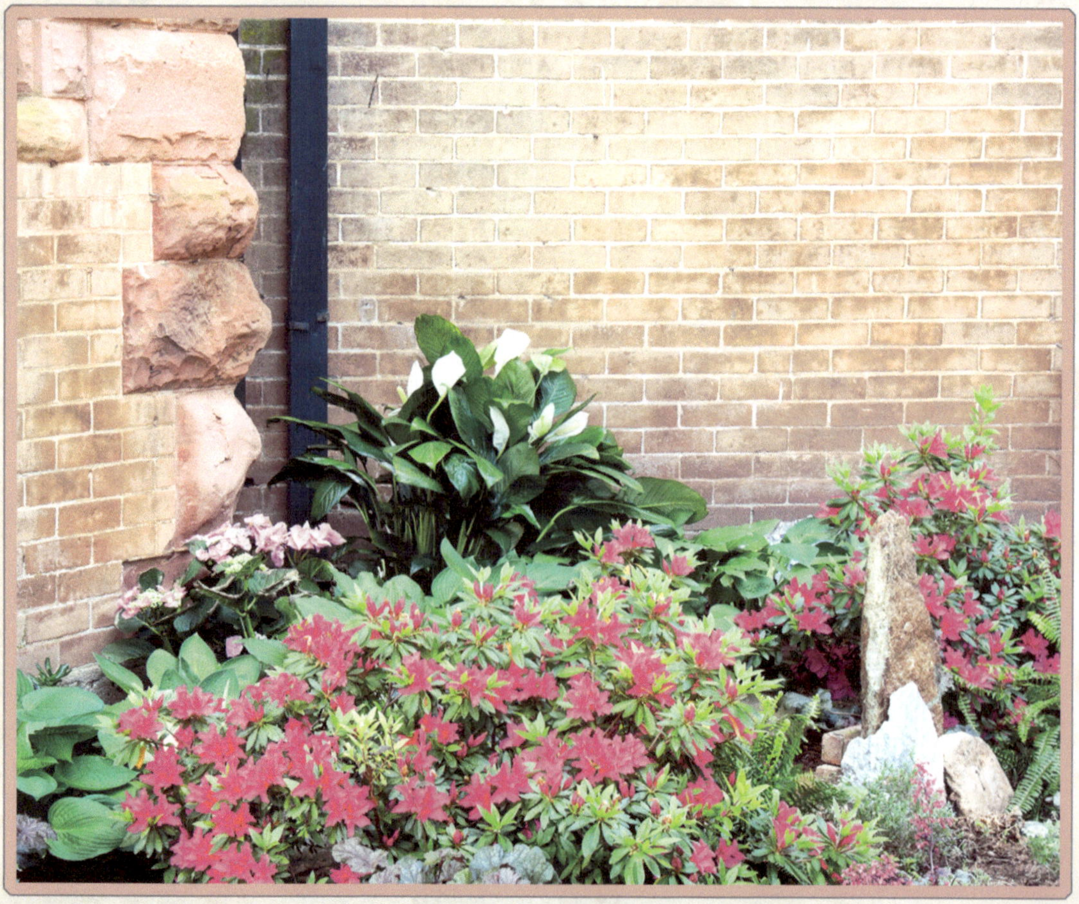

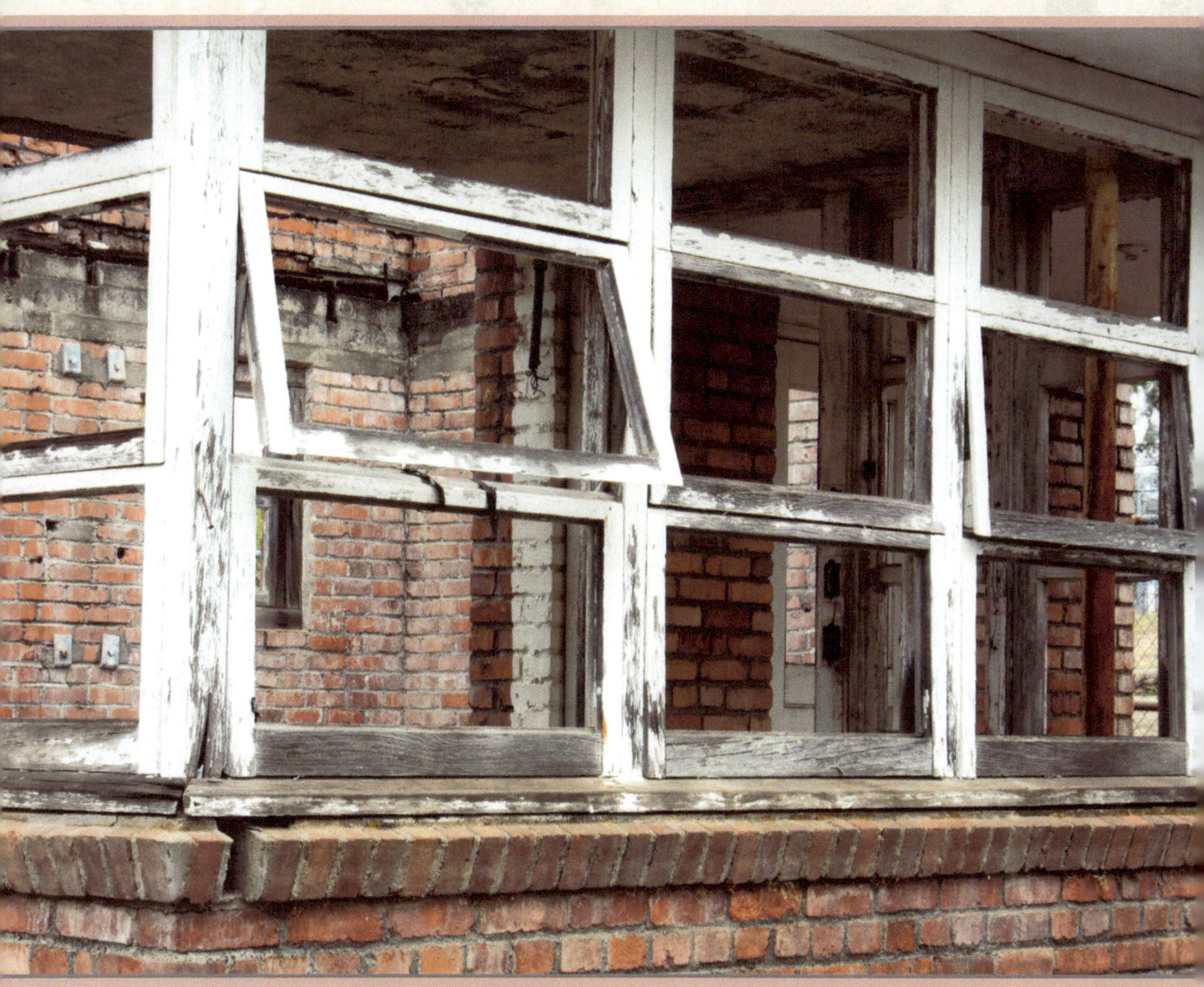

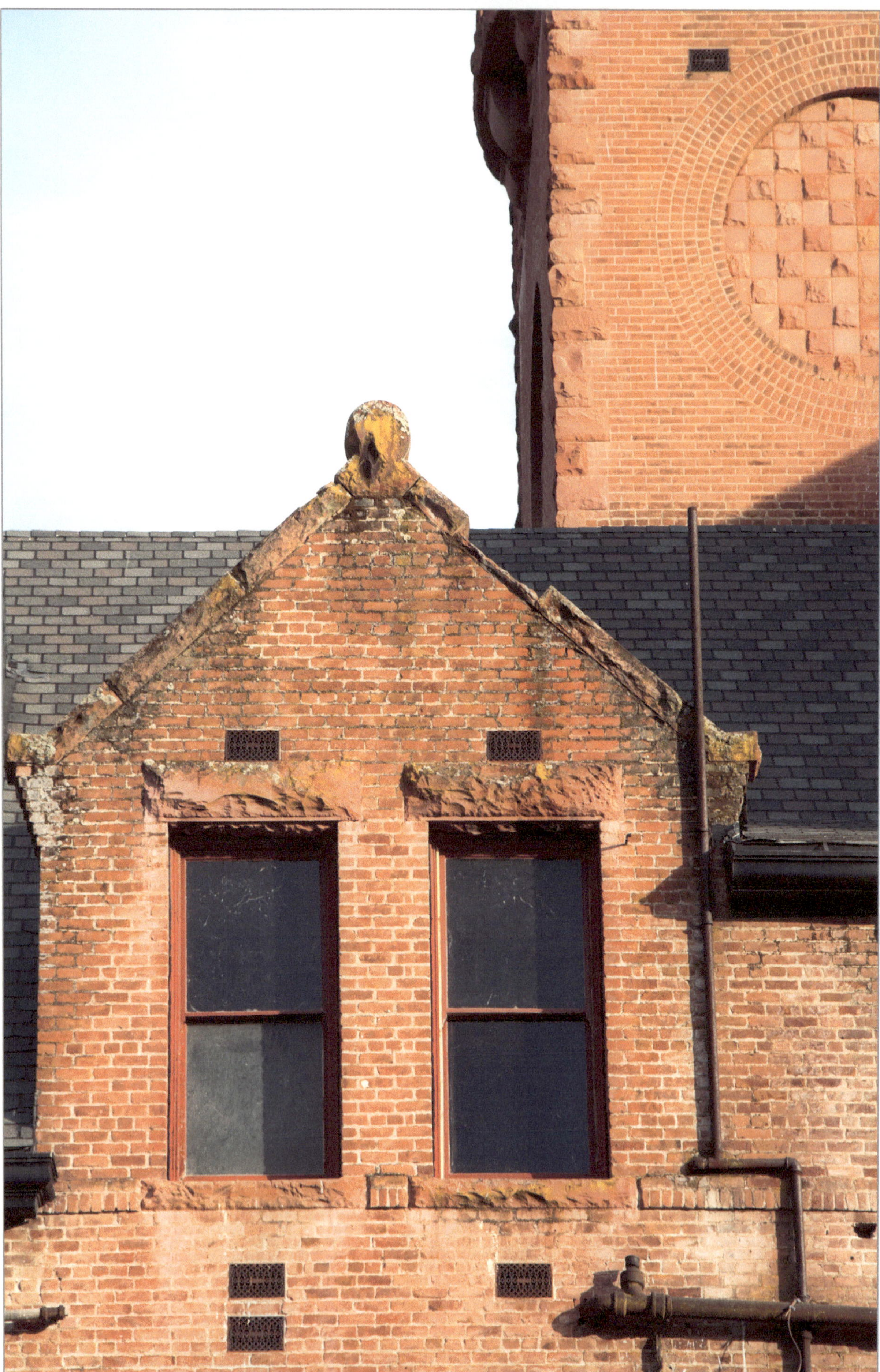

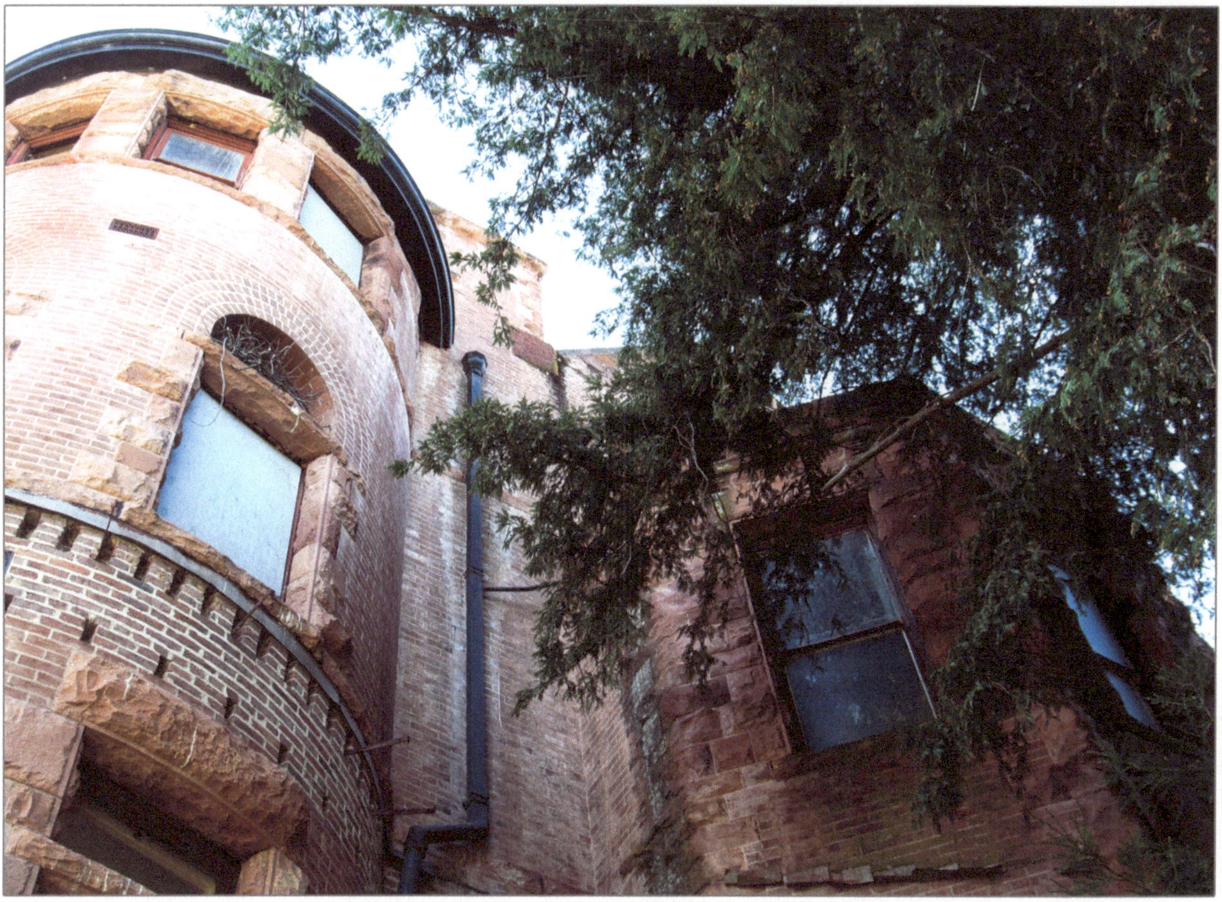

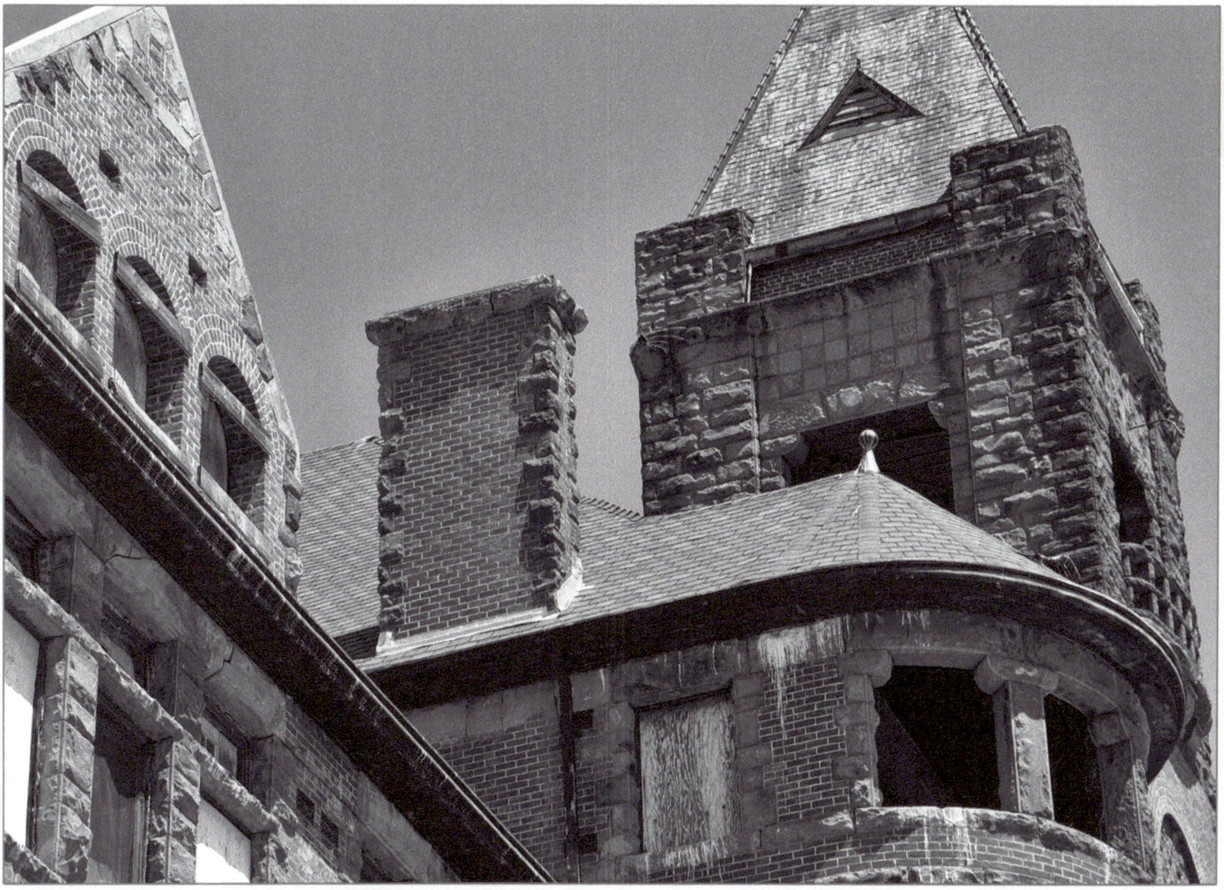

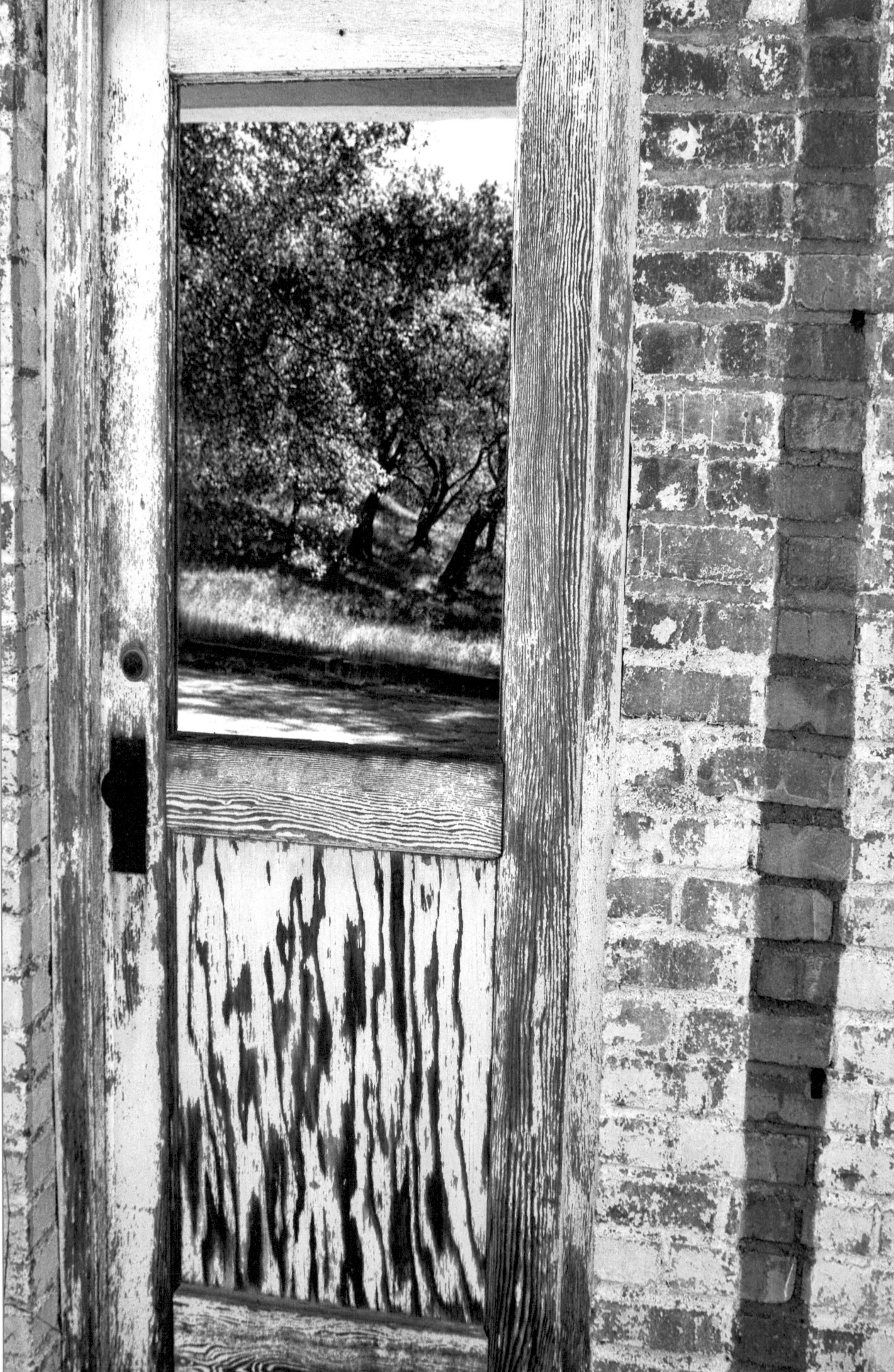